DISCOVERING NATURE WITH YOUNG CHILDREN

Funded by
MISSION COLLEGE
Carl D. Perkins Vocational and Technical Education Act Grant

discovering nature with young children

The
**Young
Scientist**
Series

Ingrid Chalufour and Karen Worth
Education Development Center, Inc.

Redleaf Press®
www.redleafpress.org
800-423-8309

Published by Redleaf Press
10 Yorkton Court
St. Paul, MN 55117
www.redleafpress.org

Written by Ingrid Chalufour and Karen Worth with Robin Moriarty, Jeff Winokur, and Sharon Grollman

This book was written with the support of National Science Foundation Grant ESI-9818737. However, any opinions, findings, conclusions, and/or recommendations herein are those of the authors and do not necessarily reflect the views of NSF.

Cover and interior design by Percolator
Interior typset in Weiss
Printed in the United States of America

Library of Congress Cataloging-in-Publication Data
Chalufour, Ingrid.
    Discovering nature with young children / Ingrid Chalufour and Karen Worth for Education Development Center, Inc.
        p. cm.—(The young scientist series)
        Includes bibliographical references and index.
        ISBN 978-1-929610-38-9
        1. Science—Study and teaching (Early childhood)—Activity programs. 2. Nature study. I. Worth, Karen.
II. Education Development Center. III. Title. IV. Series: Chalufour, Ingrid. Young scientist series.

LB1139.5.S35C43 2003
372.3'57—dc21

                                                                              2003013370

Printed on acid-free paper

contents

wk 1

wk 2

wk 3

acknowledgments

The Young Scientist Series was developed by the project staff of the Tool Kit for Early Childhood Science Education housed at Education Development Center, Inc. (EDC), with funding from the National Science Foundation.

Numerous educators and consultants contributed to the development and field testing of the series. We would like to thank the following people for their contributions to this work.

DEVELOPMENT TEACHERS

Cindy Hoisington
Lucia McAlpin
Carole Moyer
Rebecca Palacios
Susan Steinsick

PILOT TEACHERS

Colette Auguste
Liana Bond
Imelda DeCosta
Marlene Dure
Frank Greene
Karen Hoppe
Terry Küchenmeister
Stuart Lui
Maureen McIntee
Susan Miller
Katherine O'Leary
Carolyn Robinson
Ellen Sulek
Laurie Wormstead
Tiffany Young

FIELD TEST SITES

Bainbridge Island Child Care Centers, Bainbridge Island, WA
Barre Town School, Barre, VT
Berlin Elementary School, Berlin, VT
Blackwater Community School, Coolidge, AZ
Blue Hill Avenue Early Education Center, Boston, MA
Bright Horizons at Preston Corners, Cary, NC
Childspace Day Care Centers, Philadelphia, PA
City of Phoenix Head Start, Phoenix, AZ
Cisco Family Connection Bright Horizons, Milpitas, CA
East Montpelier Elementary School, East Montpelier, VT
Epic Head Start, Yakima, WA
Fort Worth Museum of Science and History, Fort Worth, TX
Four Corners School, East Montpelier, VT
K–5 Inquiry-Based Science Program, Seattle Public Schools, WA
Louisiana Tech University Early Childhood Education Center, Ruston, LA
Motorola Childcare and Education Center, Schaumburg, IL
Pasadena Unified School District, Pasadena, CA
Phoenix Head Start, Phoenix, AZ
Portage Private Industry Council Head Start, Ravenna, OH
School for Early Learning, Spring Branch Independent School District, Houston, TX
Thomson Early Childhood Center, Seattle, WA
UMC Child Development Lab, Columbia, MO
Valle Imperial Project in Science, El Centro, CA
William H. Rowe School, Yarmouth, ME
Young Achievers Science and Mathematics Pilot School, Boston, MA

ADVISORY BOARD MEMBERS

Douglas Clements
David Dickinson
George Forman
Linda French
Marilou Hyson
Stephanie Johnson
Diane Levin
Mary Jane Moran
Carolyn Vieria
Sandra Williams
Diane Willow

CONSULTANTS

Mary Eisenberg
Pat Fitzsimmons
Ben Mardell
Janet Sebell

We also would like to acknowledge the following people at EDC:

Erica Fields, Research Assistant
Kerry Ouellet, Editor and Production Manager
Susan Weinberg, Senior Administrative Assistant

introduction

"In a world filled with the products of scientific inquiry, scientific literacy has become a necessity for everyone. Everyone needs to use scientific information to make choices that arise every day. Everyone needs to be able to engage intelligently in public discourse and debate about important issues that involve science and technology. And everyone deserves to share in the excitement and personal fulfillment that can come from understanding and learning about the natural world" (National Research Council 1996, 1).

"If a child is to keep alive his inborn sense of wonder, he needs the companionship of at least one adult who can share it, rediscovering with him the joy, the excitement, and the mystery of the world" (Carson 1965).

How do we keep alive this inborn sense of wonder in early childhood classrooms? How can teachers provide children with appropriate experiences and guidance? Using the Young Scientist series is one way. But before we describe the series and how to use this guide, we would like to share a few responses to two important questions: (1) Why is science knowledge important? and (2) Why should we start in the preschool years?

Why Is Science Knowledge Important?

One goal of science is to understand the natural world. Knowing some science can help us explain why things happen, such as why water evaporates and why plants grow in particular locations, what causes disease, and how electricity works. Scientific knowledge also can help us predict what might happen—when a hurricane may hit the coast or how severe the flu will be this winter.

But science is more than knowledge; it is also a process of exploration that we call *scientific inquiry*. When scientists try to learn something about events,

objects, or materials, they observe wonder, and ask questions. And they go further and focus on one question, predicting what they think they might find out and setting up an investigation. They observe closely, using their senses and tools to collect and record data and evidence. Through analysis of their data and reflection on all they've done, they develop new ideas and theories and communicate those to others.

Most of us are not scientists, but in many small ways, we do science. When you ask the question, "How much light does my geranium need to flower well?" then test the different possibilities by putting one in the sun and one in the shade to find your answer, you are doing science. When you compare two pens, predict which one you think will work best for the drawing you are making, and then try them out, you are doing science. When you use a book to find out what kind of birdseed will attract cardinals, you are doing science.

Whether we work in a lab or a school, chart the courses of hurricanes, or want to learn about sound, we all have questions—scientists and nonscientists, adults and children alike—and we all use some of the basic tools of scientific inquiry. Given the opportunity to explore and discover, we can feel the sense of wonder, joy, and excitement that Rachel Carson describes above.

Why Should We Start Science in the Preschool Years?

Children's curiosity about the natural world, their "inborn sense of wonder," is a powerful catalyst for their work and play. With this curiosity and the need to make sense of the world, children are motivated to ask questions, explore how things work, and look closely at the natural world around them.

But in today's world, children's experiences and their opportunities to do science are often limited—confined too frequently to the passive and secondhand experience of the television or video game. Modern technology also has hidden from view some of the basic ways in which things work. Our food comes from stores and few children have seen or engaged in growing and processing it. Toys that were once pushed or pulled or rolled now have hidden motors and batteries to drive them and a switch to turn them on and off.

Science curriculum is important in the early childhood classroom so that "doing science" becomes a natural and critical part of children's early learning. With carefully selected materials and thoughtful guidance, children's explorations will encourage them to observe more closely, develop new ideas about the world, and build a foundation of experiences and ideas on which to construct later understanding. Science in early childhood classrooms also provides a rich context in which children can develop other important skills, including large- and small-muscle control, language and early mathematical understanding, and cooperation.

What Is the Young Scientist Series?

The Young Scientist series is a science curriculum for children who are three to five years old. Each of the teacher guides provides background information and detailed guidance on how to incorporate science into your daily program using many of the materials you already have in the classroom in new ways. *Discovering Nature with Young Children* is about the living things right outside the classroom door. *Exploring Water with Young Children* takes a new look at the water table and *Building Structures with Young Children* challenges children to use building materials found in the classroom to explore questions of how to make things strong,

tall, or elegant. Each study can take several months or extend over longer periods of time.

The Young Scientist series is not about learning and repeating facts, information, and vocabulary with little direct experience. It is not following a set of directed activities or learning the scientific method. It is not a week focused on bears and it is not observing random objects on a science table. The Young Scientist series makes science the work and play of exploring materials and phenomena, while providing opportunities for children to learn from that experience. Young children may do this as they engage in fantasy and dramatic play—creating magic potions at the water table or building a home for the make-believe turtle in the block area. They may do science as they challenge themselves or invent a game: "Who can build the highest tower or empty the water bucket the fastest?" They also may engage in exploration as young scientists, wondering and questioning and seeking to make sense of the world: "What would happen if I rolled the ball from the very top of the ramp? What does my worm need to live? I wonder if I can find an anthill near the one we found yesterday?"

As they explore and interact with one another, young children try to make sense of what they see and do. They develop early theories about why things are the way they are, act the way they do, and how they relate to one another. As their experience broadens and their thinking deepens, their ideas and theories become more plausible and closer to current understandings in science.

Exciting science experiences for young children do not just happen. The Young Scientist series establishes your important role to ensure that children's play and ideas about science are focused, deepened, and challenged. The following examples illustrate the differences between activity-based nature study, a thematic approach, and an in-depth exploration of the science of living things in the environment.

Teacher A takes the children out to play. A small group finds a worm and carries it over to her with great excitement. They ask if they can bring it in and the teacher agrees, sending her aide to get a small cardboard box. Scooping a bit of soil into the box, the teacher asks children to put the worm into the box. Once back in the classroom, she puts the worm in its new home on the science table and invites the "worm finders" to observe it. At circle time, she asks the group to share their story about finding the worm, then tells the class the worm will be the class pet for a few days. The next day the teacher reads *The Very Hungry Caterpillar* and asks children to compare the worm with the caterpillar in the book. She then creates a few rules for how to handle the worm and opens the table for groups of four during activity time. Over the next couple of days, different children observe and play with the worm. As their interest begins to wane, the teacher announces that together they'll put the worm outside the next day. However, she discovers she doesn't have time to return the worm with the children, and she deposits the worm in the playground herself.

In this example, the children actively enjoy playing with the worm at the science table, but opportunities for both independent and cooperative learning are limited. The worm stimulates their interest, but there is no guidance or encouragement for them to investigate ideas such as the relationship between the worm and the environment; its physical characteristics and behaviors. Children's interest and curiosity is clear, but the potential for reflection, dialogue, and developing ideas about some interesting and critical life science concepts is minimal. Moreover, there is little attention to developing children's respect for living things.

Teacher B notices the children's interest in worms and decides to do a project on worms. She gathers many materials: plastic worms for the sand table and block area; books about worms, snakes, and caterpillars along with a couple of Richard Scarry books (children love Lowly Worm); worm pictures she has found; clay for rolling worms; brown paper in the paint area for worm paintings; and a new insect puzzle with letters. She plans to use the opportunity to teach the letter *W* to the children. Teacher B introduces the project with a class discussion asking children to share their experiences with worms. She identifies the areas in the classroom where there are worm activities and encourages children to spend some time at each. During the week she moves through the classroom supporting children's play and, during group time, encourages them to talk about their worm experiences. Toward the end of the project, the children make a special trip outdoors and bring a worm back to the classroom to visit for a day.

In this example, children are surrounded with worm activities. The block area, the sand table, the art corner, and many of the choice tables have worm-related activities—all of which address basic literacy, math,

and social skills. The children are very engaged and the visiting worm is the highlight of the week. But this project with its science theme has little to do with scientific inquiry and exploration of science concepts.

Teacher C also responds to her children's interest in worms. But she decides that their interest in worms could be the beginning of an exploration of living things in the local environment. When children find a worm outside, she looks at it with the children and asks them to show her where it came from. The next day, she takes the worm finders (and a few other children who show interest) to the spot where the worm was found. There, she engages them in a dialogue about how they found the worm and where the worm lived. When children request to bring the worm in, she says it would be wonderful to have the worm in the class for a short time, but first they needed to plan for the visit. The teacher and the class talk and wonder together: What kind of home do they think the worm would need? How could they make it like his home outdoors? What might be important to remember when the worm was visiting? A couple of days later, after much discussion about the worm and its needs as well as some "research" about keeping small animals in the classroom, the children are ready to create the worm environment and they go outdoors and find a few to bring in. Over the next couple of weeks, the children carefully observe the worms as they measure them, draw pictures of them, and discuss their ideas at circle time. They explore and debate how worms move and what they eat. And then, because they are not sure that all the worms' needs are being met, the whole class goes out and carefully returns the worms to the spot from which they came.

As in the other examples, children in this classroom enjoyed playing with the worms, but in this case they are also engaged in an active, hands-on science inquiry project that illustrates the approach of the Young Scientist series. The teacher builds on the children's interests and has defined a clear set of science concepts to guide their work with living things. She encourages them to conduct their own observations and explorations. While many other skills are practiced and learned, science is in the foreground. Using the outdoor environment and indoor visitors she promotes creative, deep exploration and children's use of inquiry.

She focuses the children's attention on important concepts about living things:

- Basic needs
- Physical characteristics
- Habitats
- Behaviors

She encourages deeper thinking to enrich their experiences without interfering in their own process of questioning and exploration. As she does this the children develop their skills in the following:

- Observing closely
- Describing what they see
- Raising questions
- Investigating
- Representing things and ideas
- Discussing

And as she engages the children in planning the worm's visit to the classroom, she guides the children in the following:

- Appreciating the connection between an organism and its environment
- Appreciating the need to care for the environment
- Realizing their responsibility for the animals they bring into the classroom

As you continue to read and begin to implement, you will learn more about science for young children and what they can do. You will also learn about how to make it possible for children to engage in the rich science exploration exemplified by Teacher C. As you teach, keep in mind these basic principles in the Young Scientist series.

- All three- to five-year-olds can successfully experience rich, in-depth scientific inquiry.
- The content of the science learning draws from children's experiences, is interesting and engaging, and can be explored directly and deeply over time. Expectations are developmentally appropriate; that is, they are realistic and tailored to the strengths, interests, and needs of individual children.
- Discussion, expression, representation, and reflection are critical ways in which children make meaning and develop theories from their active work. Children learn from one another.
- Teachers can take on specific roles and use particular strategies to actively support and guide children's science learning.

Rationale and Goals

We live in a world filled with an enormous variety of living things that inhabit all kinds of environments. Even on city streets, small plants push their way up through cracks in the sidewalk, and ants appear seemingly from nowhere. Children are fascinated by living things. The teaching methods described in this book will help children expand on that fascination to become young naturalists, encouraged to see the outdoors as an authentic place to explore living things as they exist in nature and the indoors as a place to recreate small parts of the outdoors and look more closely at temporary plant and animal visitors. The emphasis of this exploration is not on naming specific living things. While knowing the names of living things makes for more efficient communication, it does little to deepen children's understanding. Instead, the specific goals of the exploration are to provide opportunities for children to

- Observe life around them more closely.
- Build an understanding about what is living and nonliving such as the characteristics and needs of living things—their life cycles, habitats, diversity and variation, and interdependence.
- Develop science inquiry skills including wondering, questioning, exploring and investigating, discussing, reflecting, and formulating ideas and theories.
- Develop scientific dispositions including curiosity, eagerness to find out, an open mind, respect for life, and delight in being a young naturalist.

The Classroom Environment

A *naturalist* is a person who studies living things, especially by direct observation of animals and plants. One of the most important roles you play in this exploration is creating an environment and culture in your classroom that supports and encourages children to be young naturalists—the classroom must convey the excitement and wonder of observing and learning about living things. Some of the characteristics of such an environment and culture follow.

A Respect for Living Things

A naturalist environment conveys an attitude of serious respect for living things and their habitats. It is a place where children are asked to think about the needs of living things and how they are met. It emphasizes learning about plants and animals in their natural environments. Outdoors this means disturbing the environment as little as possible; indoors this means moving from practices such as keeping animals as pets and growing houseplants to creating mini-environments in which living things are in as natural an environment as possible, often only for short periods of time.

An Emphasis on Inquiry

Naturalists ask questions, observe closely over time, and think about what their observations tell them. What are the special characteristics of a particular living thing? Where is a particular living thing found? Why is it found there? What are the differences between two kinds of snails? What changes are taking place? A naturalist environment encourages children to ask such questions and to try to find answers. It emphasizes the importance of gathering data through observation by having appropriate tools on hand and time to explore. The naturalist environment is full of children's ongoing dialogue and work, photographs, charts, and panels communicating the value of documentation and recording to good naturalist study.

Sharing Observations and Ideas

In a naturalist culture, children are encouraged to share their observations and ideas through small and large group discussions, and they learn to listen to what others have to say. They share their records of what they have seen; their ideas about science concepts, such as what makes something living or nonliving; and their thoughts about what different plants and animals need to survive. They learn that ideas are valued and important whether right or wrong; that people may have different ideas; and that one can learn by asking question of others. They also learn that they need to share how and why they know what they know as well as what they know.

Documentation and Recording

Naturalists spend a great deal of time documenting what they see—using careful sketches, descriptive words, and names to most accurately remember their experiences. They use their notes to reflect with others and find patterns in their observations. Young naturalists can begin to develop these skills no matter their level of development. In a naturalist environment, materials for representation are easily available and children's work is used to discuss their ideas and to stimulate more focused investigations.

A Focus on Actual Living Things

The naturalist culture emphasizes the wonder of living things as they are, not as they appear in fantasy. Therefore, the books and other resources you use are accurate in their portrayal of living things. As young naturalists, children are encouraged to try to represent what they see, not what they imagine, and to begin thinking about the needs and behaviors of living things. Fantasy certainly has its place, but is clearly distinguished from the real thing.

Children as Young Naturalists

This exploration is designed to provide experiences over time in which children can engage in multiple ways depending on who they are and what they bring. You may find that some children are immediately drawn into the exploration, constantly searching for clues about where different small animals live or how and what they eat. Other children may be more reluctant, shying away from bugs or anything that moves. Some children will quickly grasp the concepts of living and nonliving, while others struggle with these ideas. How children approach this exploration, and what they learn, is influenced by a range of factors including the different experiences, needs, skills, and ideas that young children bring. As you prepare for this exploration, you will need to consider these factors.

Prior Experiences

Young children bring to a study of living things their own ideas, interests, and beliefs based in experience and culture, and tempered by their developmental level. Some children may have had contact with many living things both in natural habitats and as part of a household of pets and plants; others may have had little contact. Some may see many organisms as dangerous or scary; others may come from cultures in which certain organisms are to be feared or revered. It is, therefore, useful to talk to children's families to learn more about children's previous experiences, interests, and fears.

DIVERSE STRENGTHS AND CHALLENGES

Any class presents you with a diverse group of children. The Young Scientist series presents an ideal curriculum for diverse classrooms. All children can explore materials and objects; all children try to make sense of their environment. Each child in your classroom can engage with science and contribute to the classroom learning whether she is three or five years old, speaks English or Spanish or Creole at home, is typically developing or has a special need.

Naturalist exploration relies heavily on observation and direct access to living things and their habitats. Be sure that all children, including those with disabilities, have opportunities to observe and explore living things. As you plan, consider environmental adaptations you may need to make (such as how to arrange the space, how to place the materials so that all children know where to find them and can access them easily, or how to provide access to outdoor settings). Also think about curriculum adaptations (such as using visual cues or body language to convey information to children whose first language is not English) and materials adaptations (such as attaching thick upright handles to tools for children with small-muscle problems) that can support children's participation. Remember, some children may not have the internal control needed to handle living things safely. For this reason, it is critical that an adult is present whenever children handle animals.

COMMUNICATION SKILLS

Central to the role of the naturalist is the close observation of living things. As with all science, describing and recording what is observed is essential. Children will have varying levels of observation, language, and representational skills depending on experience and developmental level. Some children may not have the use of many words to describe what they see but may use their bodies and actions instead. Others may draw with great detail. The drawings of others may only include one major characteristic of a living thing: for example, a line may represent a worm, or a swirl may

represent a snail. In each case, an important characteristic of the living thing guides the representation. Some children will document what they see using three-dimensional materials. It is important to encourage thinking and representation without expecting or pushing children to go beyond their capabilities.

CHILDREN'S IDEAS

Because all young children have had some experiences with living things, they all have ideas and theories about them, which may be more or less accurate. *Discovering Nature with Young Children* will give children many experiences with which to modify their ideas and theories and build new ones. But do not expect children to "correct" their initial ideas based on this exposure alone, and do not try to correct them directly. Through conversation, questions, and gentle probing, some children will come to new understandings, more reasonable, but not necessarily more accurate, than their old ones. Other children will need repeated exposure to ideas and experiences over extended periods of time to let go of old ideas and begin to refine and deepen their understanding.

The questions children have also may be very different from the ones you have. You cannot know what every child in your group is thinking, but you may get an idea of different children's points of view by listening to, questioning, and observing children as they explore. It also is helpful to think about some of the typical ideas, questions, and naïve conceptions young children have about some of the basic science concepts that are related to this exploration. You will find information about some of the more common ideas children hold in step 1 of the "Getting Ready" section (p. 13).

Science Exploration through Play

Play is fundamental to children's development, and they approach much of what they do through play. Children engage in many kinds of play, including dramatic or symbolic play, exploratory play, and constructive play (Eisenberg 2000). As young naturalists, children will be engaging in exploratory play as they look for living things, find out what they are like and what they do, examine where they live, and learn about what they need. This will help children gather information and experiences necessary to ask and pursue new questions.

You also will want to encourage symbolic play in this exploration by asking children to assume the role of the young naturalist with their own naturalist tools and other props such as hats and aprons with many pockets. They might also become creatures themselves, moving and behaving as though they were a particular animal. Symbolic play may go on in the block corner or sand table as well, with children creating homes or environments for play animals or imaginary ones. There may well be opportunities for you to join this play and engage children in discussion and activity around some of the concepts they are learning.

Many children will see the study of small animals as an opportunity to become caregivers, the animals becoming pets or substitute babies. It is important to respect children's caring but to carefully reinforce the idea that it is essential to meet the needs of living things. Looking for animals outdoors may lead some children to take on the role of hunters rather than the role of the naturalist. It is best to redirect this kind of play at this time as it may lead to rough treatment of the animals and may conflict with developing an attitude of respect for the living environment.

Children may also want to engage in constructive play with animals. Their interests can be focused on building terraria or designing a garden. They may also want to create raceways for worms or build block houses for snails. In these instances, you will need to stop the play and refocus children's attention, discussing, if appropriate, why the children cannot do these things with living creatures.

Connections between Science Outcomes and Other Domains

As you provide opportunities for children to explore living things, and guide them in their development of science inquiry skills, you will also see growth in language, literacy, mathematics, and social skills, as well as in children's approaches to learning. The chart that appears in the appendix (pp. 147–153) shows the connections between science inquiry outcomes as we define them in the Young Scientist series and the

outcomes of other subject areas taken from the Head Start Child Outcomes Framework.

Mathematics is one of the languages scientists use to record and reflect on their observations and to communicate their ideas to others. Children who are exploring living things will also become meaningfully involved with mathematics ideas as they count, measure, sort, categorize, and compare the many plants and animals in their surroundings. They will also use other mathematics skills as they look at the shapes of leaves and trees, at small animals, and for patterns.

Scientists also communicate with words. As children communicate their findings, participate in discussions, and represent their experiences, they are certainly increasing their language and literacy skills. In fact, research suggests that engaging children in rich science experiences provides a context and a purpose for meaningful language and literacy learning. By engaging with science, children build their vocabulary while developing an ability to communicate their ideas. Such a capacity for oral language provides the foundation for all literacy learning. Children also learn about the importance of books as they use them to find out what their snails need to live or to get ideas about building techniques, materials, and designs. They learn to record their observations, explanations, and ideas about how worms or snails behave by using multiple forms of representation, including drawings, simple graphs, and writing. Such representations provide a visible record that encourages children to reflect on and talk about their theories and what they have discovered.

Science is a social activity. Whether in person or through other means of communication, scientists exchange ideas, build on one another's work, and often collaborate on science investigations. As children pursue their questions about living things, they need to work together to find interesting plants and animals, build a classroom terrarium, and exchange ideas about how a snail moves or when a pill bug curls up. Together their individual ideas can suggest a bigger picture and new ideas—all things that eat are alive. Such collaborative work (that involves sharing materials and ideas) provides children with significant opportunities for developing their social skills.

Making the Most of the Curriculum

Teachers who implement the Young Scientist series will use a specific approach to teaching: a set of strategies that balance the children's rich explorations with some more structured activities. This curriculum and the many accompanying tools and resources are designed to support you as you learn to use this approach. As you prepare to implement *Discovering Nature with Young Children*, we encourage you to focus on four basic aspects of teaching that may be new to you: the science, the physical environment of the classroom, time and scheduling, and the facilitation and guidance of children's learning.

SCIENCE

You do not need to be a scientist to implement this curriculum. But in order to be responsive to children's explorations, you need to recognize and experience the science phenomena children are experiencing. There is no better way to build this understanding than to engage with the science. When you are outside helping a child find a small animal, you will be much better at guiding her if you have been looking yourself. When children raise questions about how a snail eats, your observations and reading will help you suggest what children might focus on and what you might show them in a book or tell them. You will appreciate the challenge of drawing a ladybug if you have tried it yourself. Before introducing *Discovering Nature with Young Children* to children, take time to be a naturalist yourself. You will find activities to guide you in step 1 of the "Getting Ready" section on p. 13; this section will also help you understand common ideas children have about the living things around them.

PHYSICAL ENVIRONMENT

Science for young children is about investigating real things, developing new ideas and theories, and sharing them with others. The richer and more varied the environment is, the richer and more varied the experiences the children will have. In addition, children's exploration will be more independent and sustained if the tools they need are readily available where and when they need them. You will find guidelines for setting up this environment in steps 3 and 4 of the "Getting Ready" section and in the preparation section of each step. Additional ideas are provided in the resources section.

TIME AND SCHEDULING

Scientific inquiry takes time. Going out to observe living things in the environment requires careful looking and several trips. Finding out how a worm moves means observation over a period of time and comparing movement to another animal. Planting seeds and then watching plants grow requires observations and discussions throughout the plant's life cycle. A typical schedule often does not include regular time periods of forty-five minutes to an hour and yet this is what is needed for groups of children to study something closely. Often the program calls for a new theme or topic weekly or every two weeks, but *Discovering Nature with Young Children* should go on for two to three months with some observations and activities spread out across the year. Suggestions for scheduling different activities are provided in the "Getting Ready" section and throughout the guide. You will also find suggestions for making extended study possible.

FACILITATING AND GUIDING LEARNING

With your own naturalist exploration under your belt, a physical environment that invites and supports children's inquiry, and a schedule that allows the time, the stage is set for the most important part of teaching—your interactions with the children. There may be some new strategies to learn, new expectations required, and old approaches to let go of. This guide is designed to help you become a teacher of science—engaging children in science and focusing and deepening their experiences and thinking. The step-by-step guide is designed to help you as you learn new roles and approaches.

Involve Families

Families are important to *Discovering Nature with Young Children*. In cases where parents are not the sole caregivers, you can involve a grandparent, foster parent, aunt, uncle, older sibling, or cousin. As you involve families, consider how culture might influence a child's experiences with living things. For example, some families may have a particular reverence for nature or certain animals; some families may discourage children from handling insects or other creatures; and others may come from cultures where children are expected to listen, not to question. Talk with family members to learn about their cultures and children's experiences. This knowledge will help you engage families appropriately and respectfully.

And families have much to share about their children. Individual children may have had interesting and/or problematic experiences with living things that are important to know. Some children may have pets or have had farm experiences. Others may have helped with a garden or have plants at home. Still others may have had a bad experience being bitten by a dog or stung by a bee. Families can provide you with important clues about such experiences as well as what living things intrigue their children, what questions they have, and what strategies you might use to support children's learning.

Take steps at the beginning to inform families about *Discovering Nature with Young Children*—what you will be doing, what children will learn, and why this is important for children's development. Feel free to use or adapt the sample letter on p. 131 that introduces families to the exploration. If a caregiver does not speak English, find someone to help you translate the letter or make an audiotape in their home language. Also invite families into the classroom or host a family night where families can experience firsthand the importance of your science explorations and experiment with ways to promote children's explorations of living things at home and in the community.

Be sure to let families know that their participation is welcome and needed and that you are interested in having them share their expertise as well as their concerns. Family members can be rich resources if they have cultural stories to share, experiences with raising plants and/or animals, or knowledge about places to visit. Also, encourage family members to work as classroom volunteers. Some families may be able to help in the classroom on a regular basis; others may come in just for special occasions such as field trips or special events. They can serve as invaluable assets when you take the class outdoors, providing children with the adult guidance they need to help them focus and observe more deeply. Indoors, family volunteers can assist with small group explorations and ensure that an environment of respect for living things is maintained while children's curiosity is promoted.

Let parents know what they can do at home with their children. They might look for living things in their neighborhood or plant seeds with their children. Family outings are another great way for children and families to see the science in their communities. Suggest places to go. For example, a trip to a local greenhouse or nursery can spark children's curiosity. Such activities can reinforce and extend the science children are learning in the classroom, while helping children and families see science phenomena in their daily lives. It is also helpful to provide sample questions that families can use to spark children's thinking and questions. "Discovering Nature with Families," included in the resources, offers ideas for activities and thoughtful questions that families can ask children. You might also provide families with a list of children's books that relate to the science concepts they are learning. See the "Books and Videos" section (p. 130) for some suggestions.

How to Use This Guide

Discovering Nature with Young Children includes three stages that will guide you in promoting children's exploration of living things and their use of inquiry.

GETTING READY. To facilitate this exploration, you will need to prepare. This section will help you to explore the science concepts embedded in this exploration. This section will also help you prepare the physical environment and think about routines and schedules that support children's inquiry into living things.

OPEN EXPLORATION. During this stage, children explore plants and animals, both outdoors at a local playground or park and indoors in a terrarium you create. These initial explorations are intended to encourage children to use their senses to observe living things as young naturalists by noticing and describing the physical characteristics, behaviors, and needs of livings things in their natural environments. During this stage, children will also learn to use basic tools, such as hand lenses and penlights, which will extend their senses and help them be better observers of the plants and animals around them. At this time, do not share your own ideas of what children should be noticing. Instead, encourage children to look more closely at different living things and pay attention to what they observe, what intrigues them, and what they understand about living things.

FOCUSED EXPLORATION. After children have had multiple opportunities to openly explore the characteristics, behaviors, and needs of living things in their natural environment, they are ready for focused exploration. During this stage, you encourage children to look more closely at living things, moving from descriptions of general external features to more complex observations of body parts and their functions. At the same time, you help children connect their observations of plants and animals with the environment in which they live. Your role is to deepen children's understandings by asking probing questions, encouraging children to represent their work, and creating opportunities for discussion and reflection. Extension activities—such as a field trip to a nearby bird sanctuary, sharing an interesting book or reference material, or a visit from a naturalist—take place about once a week throughout "Focused Exploration." These experiences motivate children to continue their indoor and outdoor explorations in new ways, provide new information, and/or connect their work to their lives outside of school.

"Focused Exploration" includes two different studies. The plant study focuses on plants' growth and development, the interrelatedness of their different parts, their needs, and their life cycle. This study relies on regular indoor and outdoor explorations as well as monthly observations of a tree or bush. The animal study focuses on animals' physical characteristics, behaviors and needs, and their life cycles. The animal study relies on regular explorations of animals in the indoor terrarium and outdoors in their natural habitats.

Each step of "Open Exploration" and "Focused Exploration" includes the following sections:

CORE EXPERIENCES provide a rationale for the step—the science ideas you'll be focusing on, why this is important for children, and how this step relates to the overall exploration.

The PREPARATION section will help you get ready for each step as you consider your classroom schedule, the materials you will need, what you'll need to check in the outdoor environment, and ways to connect with families.

The TEACHING PLAN offers detailed guidance for implementing the step, including what you might say and do to engage children and facilitate their explorations and help them reflect on their experiences and ideas. The left-hand column of this section guides you through the exploration. Issues teachers have raised and our responses are found in the right-hand column, which also includes photographs, drawings, and sample dialogue. This column gives a picture of what the plan looks like "in action," while suggesting ways to extend science explorations.

At the end of the section on open exploration, you will find three different types of extensions for enriching children's naturalist explorations. They include planning a field trip to explore different environments, inviting experts into the classroom, and using books and videos to extend the exploration.

The resource section provides more information about the teaching approach of *Discovering Nature with Young Children*, essential information for working with living things indoors and out; and book and video resources. We encourage you to familiarize yourself with this section before you start. You will find references to the resources throughout the guide. Some of what is there may be useful to you right away; other material may be more helpful after you have had some initial experiences teaching *Discovering Nature with Young Children*.

Worm City: Excerpts from a Teacher's Journal

These journal entries illustrate what one preschool teacher learned when she helped her children become young naturalists.

SEPTEMBER 8

Last week during circle time we talked about being naturalists. The kids were so excited at first—they loved the idea of going outdoors to observe plants and animals. We talked about what they might see and they had lots of ideas—caterpillars, worms, ants. But when they got outside, they didn't find much except for a few dead leaves. They were pretty disappointed.

Then yesterday Brent found a bunch of wormy creatures under rocks near the door. So we have a new spot for exploring, and I now have a class full of diggers!

SEPTEMBER 18

Kids were really into digging at first, but the playground was a big temptation. When the choice was to dig or to swing, digging didn't always win out. I kept thinking, "Hey, aren't my kids supposed to be naturalists? What's the matter with these kids? What's the matter with me?" I finally talked to my supervisor and she got me thinking about what I could change to get kids more involved. We came up with the idea of working in small groups and it's been great.

I got some parent volunteers to come in, and they supervised the other kids during our outdoor time. So they watched the runners and the swingers, while I spent my time with the diggers. I recorded what kids noticed. I took photos and drew pictures of the plants and animals they found. And we talked—about where spiders live, why leaves get brown, how worms move. The other day Brent held a squiggly worm in his palm and announced, "my worm is alive." I asked how he knew. He said, "Because it's struggling."

SEPTEMBER 23

During circle time, I asked the kids who've been focusing on outdoor explorations to share what they've found and where they found them. These conversations invite other kids in, so my group of young naturalists is growing. I'm also teaching the kids how to use tools. It took a lot of practice for them to get the hang of it, but they're finally figuring out how to hold the hand lens and look through it at the same time (no easy task), how to use a penlight and a trowel. They're seeing more, noticing more.

SEPTEMBER 30

The kids have all of these ideas about living things—some accurate, some inaccurate—and it's hard, because I'm not always sure how to respond. I've been talking to my supervisor about it, and I'm learning to see what my task is. It's not to correct kids but, rather, to use words, pictures, and drawings to bring their ideas back to them. And by bringing in resources and offering new experiences, kids can explore their ideas and check them out.

OCTOBER 4

I've been looking at all the photos of my young naturalists, and as I look, I always ask, "Why don't I have pictures of Elaine or of Andrew?" because that's very telling about kids and about myself as a teacher. By seeing which kids don't appear in those photos, I can see who hasn't been engaged. At the beginning of our study, the younger kids in the class were noticeably absent, but that's beginning to change. At this point, it seems like all the kids are involved at some level. The younger kids are into who's the mommy and daddy and baby worm. The children who are learning English are exploring just like the others, and they're learning some new words as well! There are a bunch of kids who are engaged with worms in a more focused way—measuring them, drawing them, and thinking about how they move. I think it's time to figure out how to narrow the study, to move on to a deeper investigation of living things.

OCTOBER 10

We're really beginning to focus on the basic needs of worms—observing them outdoors in their natural habitats to figure out what they need to survive. And now we're building a terrarium so we can bring the worms indoors, and that's generated a lot of excitement. Tomorrow, I'll take a small group to the big park to look for worms and to collect leaves for the terrarium.

OCTOBER 11

Eddie was in charge of pulling the wagon to the big park (that's his regular job). Kids were really attentive. I noticed Terry stopping when she spotted a stone wall and when I asked her what she was doing, she said, "Lookin' for snails," since that's where some kids had found snails before. As we got closer to the park, the kids noticed a sound. One of the kids said it sounded like bells. Then we stopped and they figured out it was coming from a wind chime. Then we waited and listened and thought about why sometimes it chimed—and sometimes it didn't. Alyssa said, " 'Cause of the wind," and just then there was a gust of wind and her hair started to blow. Alyssa laughed and said, "And it's blowing my hair, too."

On our way to the park, the kids also noticed lots of dead worms. (It had poured the day before.) I asked how they knew they weren't alive and they said, "They're not moving." "They're not in the ground." Then I asked why there were so many dead ones and Eddie said, " 'Cause someone shot them." Alyssa said her mother said it was because of the rain. (It struck me then that kids' conversations about living things don't just take place within the classroom, but also at home. It also struck me how we've created a whole culture of inquiry. It seems like wherever kids are—in the classroom, in the park, or just walking somewhere—they are so attuned to what's around them, and there's always a sense of wonder, a sense that there's something to examine and investigate and discover.)

At the park, most of the small group dug for worms and collected leaves. (Some of the kids were sidetracked on this windy day by the blowing leaves; they just wanted to run and jump in them.) The diggers talked about the worms—what they looked like, their color, their length—and how many they had collected (twenty-seven total!). Eddie was into collecting rocks. (He managed to put a big boulder into the wagon. Later he told me that the rock was too big for the terrarium; it would squish the worms, so he wanted to cut it up into little pieces of clay and then put it in the terrarium. I might follow up on that at another time—the concept that rocks could be turned into clay.) At the park, kids drew pictures of the worms and leaves.

Then they told me about the pictures, and I wrote the words down: "The worm hides under the leaves." "Worms are long." "Here is the daddy worm."

October 12

During circle time, we all counted the worms we found in the park and put them in the terrarium. Eddie said we should call our terrarium "Worm City." He then said we should put a lot of leaves on top because there were lots of leaves in the wormhole.

Kids then broke up for some free play. It was interesting that the kids who had done the collecting were "wormed out" for the moment, and went off to other areas of the classroom. Other kids now seized the opportunity to spend some time with the worms, and each kid spoke a different language. One spoke Spanish. Another spoke Arabic. Another spoke Russian. I sat around the terrarium with them. I pointed to a worm wiggling in the dirt and said, "Look how it moves." After we observed for a while, I asked, "Can you show me with your body how the worm moves?" Vanessa got on the floor. First, she stretched out, then pulled her legs in. "Like this," she said proudly.

Then Anthony saw the worm burrowing into the dirt, he said "It's going downstairs." (The Spanish word "abajo" means down and downstairs.) Anthony had kept calling worms "snails," but today he got it (!!). They were worms, and that was a big leap for him. He drew a picture of a worm and dictated a caption in Spanish that the parent volunteer recorded.

When lunch arrived, the kids were reluctant to leave the terrarium so I put the terrarium in the middle of their lunch table so they could watch the worms while they ate.

One child wondered aloud, "Think worms like ice cream?" Another said, "They eat leaves, silly." Another said, "It's berries they like." I wrote down their ideas . . . and so a new investigation begins.

October 16

During circle time, I shared children's theories about what worms eat. Then I asked the group, "So how can we find out if they eat ice cream? How would we know if they like leaves?"

As a group, we decided to observe worms in their natural habitat, checking out what is available for them to eat. We are also going to put different foods in the terrarium (though we'll skip the ice cream!), to test out kids' ideas. I'll also bring in some nonfiction books about worms, so kids can compare their discoveries to what they find in books. I've learned to take children's lead, using their theories as a starting point, then helping them think about how they might test out those theories. And by helping them test their theories, they're able to refine their thinking, and develop new theories that lead to new questions and deeper investigations.

References

Carson, Rachel. 1965. *The sense of wonder.* New York: Harper & Row.

Eisenberg, M. 2000. The influence of materials on children's play: Explorations at the water table. Unpublished study, Tufts University.

National Research Council. 1996. *National science education standards.* Washington, D.C.: National Academy Press.

getting ready

Step 1: Preparing Yourself—Science

Whether you are a gardener or have had little experience growing plants, or whether you are a pet lover or feel uncomfortable around bugs and other animals, you can become a naturalist with your children. This section will provide you with basic experiences and understandings that prepare you for helping children explore important science ideas about the world of living things. All you need is an outdoor area, a hand lens, a notebook and pencil, and a willingness to explore and wonder. In this step, you will also learn about some of the ways young children often think about these science ideas. Understanding their point of view can help you decide what experiences to provide or what to focus their attention on or the questions and responses that might further challenge their thinking.

TEACHING PLAN

Take a "naturalist" walk in a park, your neighborhood, or your backyard. On your walk, take a hand lens, a clipboard with some paper, and a field guide for your local area, if you have one. What do you see? What is living and what is not? It seems obvious to adults, but the understanding of what makes something alive is a basic concept of life science.

All things on earth are either *living* or *nonliving*. All living things share certain characteristics that become more evident as we acquire experience with the natural world. Interesting misunderstandings about this concept abound. A leaf that falls from a tree was alive and is now dead. Think about a category of things that were alive to distinguish them from things, such as a stone, that were never alive. As you explore your environment, make some lists and categories of what you see. What is alive? What was once alive? What was never alive?

Stop and look closely at the plants. Turn over a stone, log, or pile of leaves and see what you find. Pick out a small area where there are

---

TEACHER NOTE: *MONDAY*
I took a walk around my neighborhood to see what living things I could find. I found trees (maple, oak, beech, and three that I couldn't identify). I also saw many weeds (dandelions, crabgrass, and lots of others that I couldn't identify—most were grasslike).

Children ages three through five are beginning to construct their own criteria for what makes something living or nonliving. For instance, if they believe that movement is a characteristic of living things, many young children will insist that the wind or a mechanical toy is living. The greater the variety of living things they encounter and the more guidance they have in thinking about what makes things living, the more likely they are to add new criteria, such as growth, development, and reproduction, as well as the need for food and respiration.

living things. Try to become knowledgeable about the kinds of living things you come across by referring to your field guide to help you with identification and with the habits and needs of each of these living things. Remember, while the name of a living thing can help you find more information and talk with others about what you've seen, knowing what it looks like, what it needs, what is its habitat, and what it does are more important than its name.

Careful observation is not always easy or natural for adults. Sketching will force you to look more closely. Choose a living thing and sketch it. Have you learned anything new about the living thing by observing and drawing it? As you look closely, what do you notice about the *basic characteristics* of these living things (color, size, body structure)? Use your hand lens. What else can you see? Sketch again. Do you see any relationship between the living things' structures and where they are located or how they behave?

Step back from your close observation of one living thing and look at its surroundings. In order to survive, grow, develop, and reproduce, living things must meet their basic needs. Animals need food, water, and oxygen. They need space in which to live, and many of the animals we come across need light. Plants, too, need food but can make it themselves using the energy from light, water, and carbon dioxide. They also need oxygen and space in which to grow.

As you study the surroundings, can you tell how your living thing or others meet their needs? Where do they find all they need to stay alive? All living things live in a particular environment and each has its own habitat. The *habitat* is the part of the total environment that a living thing uses to meet all its basic needs. The habitat of a squirrel may include a number of trees in a park, the ground beneath them, and the little pond nearby. The habitat of a worm in that same park may be a very small patch of earth. The pigeons in the trees may have a habitat that includes the nearby baseball stadium where they find food after ball games. People's habitats have become enormous since we no longer grow our own food but buy it in stores that import from around the world, and we get our water from reservoirs miles away. As a result, a living thing's habitat may be barely adequate.

Another question you can ask yourself as you look at living things is whether they depend on one another in any way. Did you see squirrels in trees? Did you see worms in the soil? Were bees carrying pollen from one flower to another? Critical to understanding the living world is the exploration of the *interdependence* of living things— most are dependent on others. Squirrels in the park gather nuts and seeds to eat, often hiding them in holes in the ground. The forgotten ones are planted and grow into trees. Worms make their way through the soil, making it lighter and richer so that plants can grow and other organisms can burrow easily. Human beings depend on a range of plants and animals for food and, in earlier times, were dependent on animals and plants for clothing and shelter. All living things need the oxygen emitted by plants and those same plants need the carbon dioxide exhaled from animals.

Can you find more than one example of a living thing? How many different kinds of living things can you find? There is tremendous

Young children are likely to think that an animal's needs and behaviors are similar to their own, believing that snails are looking for their parents or that worms love ice cream. Observing the natural world up close and caring for living things help children broaden and deepen their understanding of the differences and similarities in the needs of different living things and how they are met.

diversity of living things on Earth. Even within the confines of a vacant lot or backyard, many species of plants and animals live—each in its own habitat, using the resources very differently. If you look closely in a simple patch of weeds, you'll find many different kinds of plants. Turning the soil will likely result in the appearance of a number of different insects and other bugs. If you look closely at one kind of living thing, you will see the *variation* as well. All worms are not alike; neither are all squirrels. We take the idea of variation for granted when we think of human beings, dogs, and cats. But plants and other animals vary too.

Once you get started, you may spend a while simply observing living things around you, enjoying an increasing ability to notice what exists in your surroundings. Take notes and keep sketching. But nature study is more than observations: it is also thinking about what you see and trying to answer questions such as where are particular living things located (in dark or light, wet or dry)? What kinds of places seem to have the most living things? What patterns can we see?

You can learn different things about living things if you can observe them closely over time. Pick a small plant or animal to bring indoors as a temporary "visitor." What are its basic needs? How will it survive indoors for a few days? Can you create a temporary habitat? Bring the plant or animal in and take care of it for three to four days, then return it where you found it. What did you learn about this living thing by taking care of it indoors?

You can go still deeper. All living things have a *life cycle* that includes a beginning (birth for animals and germination for plants), growth, development, and death. All living things also reproduce, creating a cycle that maintains the species. Depending on when you look, you will see living things at different stages in their life cycles, but you may be able to see more than one of these stages if you pick out a particular outdoor space and return frequently. You may also find animals that can live indoors for a short time while you observe them growing, developing, and if you're lucky, reproducing. Or you may sprout and grow seeds indoors. With certain conditions, you may be able to observe the entire life cycle of a plant from seed to seed.

Step 2: Preparing Yourself—The Guide

This teacher's guide offers detailed, step-by-step guidance on how to prepare and implement each step. Read it through before you begin.

TEACHING PLAN

Read the guide carefully. The left-hand column guides you through the exploration. The right-hand column shows what the plan looks like in action; it contains issues teachers have raised with corresponding suggestions, photographs, drawings, sample charts, brief dialogue transcripts, and ways you might extend children's science explorations.

In addition to the step-by-step direction, the guide includes a section of extensions, which has suggestions for planning field trips to

As children explore living things in their own surroundings, they will begin to develop an understanding of habitats and environments and how different living things meet their needs. While they may find stories about very different environments interesting—the arctic tundra, the rainforest, or the desert—they are more likely to understand the implications for living things in those environments after becoming familiar with the living things in their own environment.

TEACHER NOTE: *MONDAY*
I actually sat down and looked closely at a patch of grass about one foot on each side of me. It is fascinating to look up close at one area like that for a while. I counted seven different plants.

Young children are certainly aware of their own changes, such as growing taller, growing older, and maturing. Some may have had experiences with pets or plants and know they, too, grow bigger and older. They also may have experiences with birth and death. But given their sense of time and their focus on the immediate, young children are unlikely to have an understanding of the life cycle or that all living things go through similar stages or that death is final. Yet, children can talk about some of the stages and observe the appearance of baby snails; meal worms changing to beetles; and plants growing, flowering, and making seed pods. If living things die, take the opportunity to discuss death as a natural part of the life cycle.

explore different environments, inviting experts into the classroom, and using books and videos. The resources section provides more information about science teaching, observation and assessment, essential information for working with living things indoors and out, strategies for involving families, and book and video resources.

Step 3: Preparing the Physical Environment—Materials and Resources

Finding the places where your children can explore living things is fundamental to this exploration. Tools and resources must be collected and available before you start. In this step you will do the following:

- Identify a nearby outdoor environment for children to explore.

- Prepare an indoor environment for exploring living things (terrarium); prepare an outdoor environment for attracting living things (compost heap).

- Collect and inventory young naturalist tools.

- Collect and inventory art and writing materials children can use to represent and describe their observations of living things.

- Collect and inventory books, videos, and posters related to plants and animals.

TEACHING PLAN

Use the classroom environment checklist on p. 139 to help you find outdoor space for the exploration, inventory classroom materials, set up your classroom, and plan your schedule.

1. Be certain that children will be able to explore an outdoor environment for living things. Explore a nearby outdoor environment (many schoolyards are fine), and note the kinds of living things children are likely to find there. Look for the following:

- Small animals, such as snails, ants, pill bugs, and/or worms (check under piles of old leaves, under or in logs, on or near trees)

- Larger animals, such as birds and squirrels

- Plants, such as flowers, weeds, seedlings, bushes, and trees

2. If you have difficulty finding animals and plants after looking carefully around school grounds, locate a spot in a quiet, preferably shady area where you can begin a compost heap. Moisten the earth around the area well. Place either a piece of wood or a pile of leaves directly on the moistened ground, and then wet the leaves or wood. If you keep the area wet, in about a week (but even better if you can wait two or three weeks), you should notice some evidence of animals—most likely worms, pill bugs, or ants. (See "Creating an Open Compost Heap," p. 122.)

Young children certainly categorize things in their world. There are bugs, flying things, trees, and birds. Their categories are built on their own criteria—what is important to them. Research (Bell 1981; Bell and Barker 1982; Osborne and Freyberg 1985) has indicated that children tend to have varying ideas about living things and how they are grouped. For example, in one survey, almost all five-year-olds said that cows are animals but that spiders and people are not. Similarly, young children often do not think that trees are plants, but rather distinctly different organisms. As children focus more closely on living things by describing and representing them and as they explore one kind of living thing, they will notice variation: not all worms are exactly alike; two flowers on the same plant do not look exactly the same.

TEACHER NOTE: *TUESDAY*
I saw a lot of ants on the playground today. I can't tell whether they are all the same or different kinds. They seem to vary in size, yet they're the same color and shape.

TEACHER NOTE: *THURSDAY*
I've decided to plant some seeds so I can observe the life cycle of a plant. I have a small garden, but I've always bought little plants. This time I'm going to do it myself and see if I can grow one from a seed!

Another way to introduce living things into a barren area is to plant some easy-to-grow things in boxes or tubs, or transplant others from a nearby yard or park.

3. Make a terrarium for your classroom so that children can explore living things indoors during choice time. Be sure that the animals you put in the terrarium can survive in that habitat. (See pp. 123–125 for instructions.)

    Before starting "Focused Exploration: Plants," collect materials for growing plants, pp. 127–129.

    Likewise, before starting "Focused Exploration: Animals," collect materials for making a terrarium for visiting animals, pp. 123–127.

4. Collect naturalist tools.

    Each child needs the following:

    - Hand lens
    - A few tongue depressors
    - Clipboard (Option: cardboard with a bulldog clip attached)
    - Pencil, ideally attached to clipboard by Velcro fastener or string (Some classes might prefer shorter, stubbier writing implements.)

    Each group of four children needs the following:

    - Hand trowel
    - Penlight or other small flashlight
    - Container for safely collecting living things
    - Piece of Plexiglas, approximately 8 by 11 inches

    The class needs the following to share:

    - Two or more empty large terrariums (one for the teacher-made terrarium and one for the children's animal terrarium)
    - Plant sprayer
    - Measuring tapes or a ball of string
    - Field guides of local plants and animals
    - Still camera and/or video camera, if possible

5. Collect as many of the following art materials as possible so that children will have opportunities to record and represent what they discover:

    - Crayons and markers (both fine and thick point)
    - Paints
    - Clay or plasticine
    - Collage materials
    - Bendable wire

TEACHER NOTE: *FRIDAY*
It's hard to really know how some things get what they need. It's easier with plants, but I was surprised where I found some of them:

- Little weeds in tiny cracks in the pavement
- A little plant actually growing out of a wall
- Some weeds way back in an alley next to a trash area

While a terrarium provides children with an environment to observe, on its own the experience is not nearly as powerful as exploring outdoors. Even if the outdoor area is small and thin on living things, use it.

TEACHER NOTE: I planned to have the class look around the school grounds for living things, but I took a look myself and noticed there was very little to see. I talked to the custodian who helped me set up a compost heap in a quiet corner. I can't wait to see what kinds of bugs we attract!

High-quality, easy-to-use tools will help children explore the plants and animals around them. It is better to have four good hand lenses that young children can easily see through and carry, than six bad ones that are scratched or too small. Good tools also help children become independent learners. For example, children can use sprayers to independently water plants, and sturdy, lightweight clipboards to regularly document their observations.

6. Collect other resources related to living things, particularly those that relate to the plants and animals children are likely to find:

- Books, including field guides for local plants and animals
- Posters
- Web sites about living things

See "Books and Videos" (p. 130) for specific suggestions.

Step 4: Preparing the Physical Environment—Classroom Set-Up

Once you have collected materials and found an outdoor area for your young naturalists to explore, you need to think about how to create an indoor environment that motivates and supports young naturalists as they do the following:

- Observe, explore, and care for different types of plants and animals
- Grow a variety of plants
- Use resource materials and naturalist tools
- Represent and reflect on their explorations of living things
- Share and analyze their observations and theories

TEACHING PLAN

1. Organize your classroom to provide children with the following:

- *Opportunities to care for and observe plants and animals*
  You will need small containers, living plants, and shelf or table space on which to set up two terraria—one for open exploration and one for focused exploration. The space cannot be too hot or cold. A shelf at child height can be useful but limits the number of children that can observe at one time. You can place the terrarium on a table or on the floor when a group wants to observe it more closely. This allows them to see it from all sides, sit and talk about or draw what they see, or use reference books to identify and learn more about what is in their terrarium. (See pp. 123–125 for further information about setting up terraria.)

- *Access to tools*
  Hand lenses or tabletop magnifiers for more careful viewing, tongue depressors for probing, plates or Plexiglas on which to place the plants or animals

- *Access to materials for drawing, writing, modeling, and collage*
  Pencils, markers, paper, clay

2. Organize your classroom display spaces to provide children with the following:

Documenting what they've seen and representing their ideas will help children to reflect on their experiences and deepen their understanding. A rich array of art materials will provide opportunities for two- and three-dimensional representation.

ISSUE: *I don't think the field guides I have are appropriate for young children. After all, they're geared for adults.*

RESPONSE: It's certainly true that children will not be able to read or understand the information in adult field guides. But when you look at field guides with children, you are modeling how to use books to find things out. Children will also enjoy looking and talking about the pictures with you, and you can read or paraphrase certain parts of the text to help them learn more. You might even point out particular words such as *tree* or *leaf*.

ISSUE: *How will I find space?*

RESPONSE: Finding extra space in classrooms is difficult. Teachers notice that children really get involved in explorations when they find living things in many areas of the classroom, so it's worth clearing whatever surfaces and shelves you can. You might want to make more room for living things by putting away some classroom materials during focused exploration.

ISSUE: *I have no wall space.*

RESPONSE: Finding places to post and display children's work, documentation panels, or photographs can be a real challenge. Some teachers have found display space on the backs of cupboards and doors or on large pieces of cardboard. They found that these displays allowed children important opportunities to share their explorations and revisit their work.

- Wall space at children's eye level on which to hang their drawings and paintings, as well as pictures or posters of living things

- A selection of books related to living things (See "Books and Videos," pp. 130–136)

3. Place a selection of books in the book area and others about the animals and plants living in it near the terrarium.

Step 5: Long-Term Planning

Discovering Nature with Young Children has many parts. You may chose to do some or all of them. You may focus intensively on this study at some points during the year and not so much at others. Here are some suggestions for some things to think about as you plan this study.

- *Observing a tree or bush each month throughout the year*
  By beginning these monthly observations from the start of the school year, children have opportunities to notice as much change as possible.

- *Exploring the outdoors*
  The study calls for outdoor exploration two or three times a week when children are fully focused on this study. By continuing to explore outdoors at least once every week or two you give children opportunities to see what happens to local plants and animals over a long period of time and during seasonal changes. Buds and flowers appear in the spring; seeds appear in the fall. These can be compared to the growth of flowers and seed studied indoors.

- *Exploring the indoor terrarium*
  By keeping your terrarium going all year long, children who are interested can continue to observe what is happening. Children can continue to compare what they are seeing indoors with the outdoor environment.

- *Observing plants indoors*
  It takes time for plants to grow and change. By beginning plants early in the school year and maintaining them, you give children opportunities to closely observe growth and development, and possibly the full life cycle.

- *Observing animals indoors*
  It takes time for animals to grow and change. If you raise painted ladies, for example, it will take close to a month for the caterpillar to become a butterfly. You may want to do this at a time when the children can observe similar organisms outdoors.

EXAMPLE: These sample year-long schedules illustrate the different ways three teachers incorporated *Discovering Nature with Young Children* into their school calendars.

Sample Calendar 1 (All parts)

SEPTEMBER
- Begin open exploration
- Begin tree study

OCTOBER
- Begin "Focused Exploration: Plants": Start plants and observe early growth and development

- Begin "Focused Exploration: Animals": Bring worms indoors and observe body parts and movement

- Continue tree study

- Continue explorations of outdoor area and indoor terrarium

NOVEMBER–MARCH
- Continue tree study

- Continue explorations of outdoor area (until it freezes) and indoor terrarium

APRIL–MAY
- Continue tree study

- Continue explorations of outdoor area and indoor terrarium

- "Focused Observation: Plants": Parts and life cycle

- "Focused Observation: Animals": Body parts, behaviors, and life cycles of long-term visiting animals

- Invite families in to see mural and class book

continues. . .

TEACHING PLAN

Review the parts of discovering nature.

OPEN EXPLORATION

These explorations of the outdoor environment and the indoor terrarium occur two or three times a week and last for a few weeks, or until children develop an interest in a focused exploration.

THE TREE/BUSH STUDY

These monthly observations ideally begin in September. Children create a class book to document the study.

ONGOING EXPLORATIONS OF THE OUTDOOR AREA AND THE INDOOR TERRARIUM

These explorations occur two or three times a week at the terrarium and outdoors, depending on the weather and the season. They provide opportunities for children to relate their focused explorations of plants and animals to the plants and animals they are getting to know over time outdoors and in the terrarium.

FOCUSED OBSERVATION: PLANTS

This focus begins with children starting a variety of indoor plants and is best done at the beginning of the school year. That way, children may have the opportunity to observe plants throughout the school year and, hopefully, to see some go from seed to seed. The remainder of the focused exploration of plants can last anywhere from four weeks to all year and involve studying plants' needs, their parts, as well as how and why they grow and develop in the outdoor environment and in the classroom.

FOCUSED OBSERVATION: ANIMALS

This focus begins with an outdoor search for small animals. In most parts of the country this focus needs to begin in the early fall or in the spring. If it begins in the fall, it can last all year, or it can stop for awhile and then resume again in the spring. The focus on animals encourages children to observe and think about ways animals' bodies and behaviors help them meet their needs. Ideally, you'll want children to experience animals' life cycles, too, which means you'll need to introduce some animals as long-term visitors in plenty of time for the children to observe a life cycle.

Sit with your school-year calendar and block the time you will need to facilitate discovering nature. See the introduction on p. 4 for a rationale for using this curriculum to meet literacy and math goals.

**Sample Calendar 2
(All parts except for "Focused Exploration: Animals")**

SEPTEMBER
- Begin open exploration

OCTOBER
- Begin "Focused Observation: Plants": Start plants and observe early growth and development
- Begin tree study
- Continue explorations of outdoor area and indoor terrarium

NOVEMBER–DECEMBER
- Continue tree study
- Continue explorations of outdoor area and indoor terrarium
- Begin "Focused Observations: Plants": Plant parts
- Begin "Focused Observations: Animals": Terrarium animals

JANUARY–JUNE
- Continue tree study
- Continue explorations of outdoor area and indoor terrarium

**Sample Calendar 3
(All parts of "Discovering Nature," but in different order)**

SEPTEMBER
- Begin open exploration
- Begin bush study

OCTOBER–MARCH
- Continue bush study
- Continue explorations of outdoor area and indoor terrarium
- Begin "Focused Observations: Animals": Body parts, behaviors, needs, and life cycle; outdoors and indoors

APRIL
- Continue bush study

continues...

Step 6: Classroom Schedule and Routines

Children need time to be able to explore. You may need to adjust your schedule for this exploration to give them that time. Establish simple rules and routines for yourself and the children so that the time is well used.

TEACHING PLAN

1. Review your schedule. Make time for the following:

- 20–30 minutes outdoor exploration, twice per week
- 5–10 minutes before each choice time to prepare children for exploration
- 30–45 minutes of choice time, at least three times per week (Be sure to include opportunities for children to explore the terrarium during this time.)
- 10–15 minutes for a meeting with whole group, at least once per week

2. Review your safety procedures for exploring living things.

- Be sure that the areas where children explore are free of glass, poison ivy, and other potential safety hazards, such as swings. (See "Safety" on p. 121.)
- Consider how to keep the plants and animals safe as children explore. Think about ways to help children understand that plants and animals are living things and need to be treated with respect. Also think about ways to help children understand the differences between playing outside and being a naturalist.
- Some children may have allergies. Be sure to check with their families.

3. Be prepared to observe children's indoor and outdoor explorations and record what you notice.

- Schedule times that you can observe children's explorations for about ten minutes, two or three times per week. When you have other adults available to help, plan activities where other children can work or play independently.
- Read the observation and assessment section (p. 119). Prepare a clipboard so you can easily record your observations of children's indoor and outdoor explorations.

- Continue explorations of outdoor area and indoor terrarium
- Begin "Focused Observation: Plants": Start plants and observe early growth and development

MAY–JUNE
- Continue bush study
- Continue explorations of outdoor area and indoor terrarium
- Continue "Focused Observation: Plants": Parts, growth, and development

---

ISSUE: *I am worried we will not be able to go outside much because of bad weather.*

RESPONSE: If the weather does not cooperate, involve children in observing the terrarium during choice time. (Whether children explore indoors or outdoors, choice time can always provide opportunities to observe living things.)

We use the term *choice time* to mean the time during the day when children are working in small groups or individually on a variety of activities. Some people call this time *activity time, center time, play time,* or *work time.*

ISSUE: *I can't focus so much of the children's time on science because they have other things to learn.*

RESPONSE: *Discovering Nature with Young Children* provides opportunities for children's physical, social, and cognitive development, as well as for language and math development. When teachers sit down to study their program goals and outcomes, they will see many connections between inquiry skills and outcomes in other domains. (See the introduction on p. 4)

Step 7: Families

By the time they start your class, children have already had many experiences and formed numerous ideas about living things. Connecting with families as you get started will allow you to build on children's life experiences and use family resources. It will also help you build a partnership with families with the goal of engaging their children in science inquiry.

TEACHING PLAN

Send a letter to families that describes the important science understandings children will develop as they become naturalists. There is a sample letter to families on p. 131 in the resource section; you can adapt it to fit your circumstances and your families.

Also, provide families with tips for exploring outdoors and indoors with their children by sending home the "Families Discovering Nature" handout on p. 132. Preview the suggestions described in the "Connect with Families" sections at the beginning of each step of open and focused exploration in the teacher's guide for specific ways you can partner with families around their children's science learning.

- Check the children's health records for allergies.

- Find out who might volunteer or who has skills and experience to share with the class.

- Consider asking families to volunteer to care for short- and long-term visiting animals and plants over weekends or during vacations.

- Make a list of ways families can help in the classroom. You might want to post this list in the classroom so families are reminded that their help is welcome.

- Set up a bulletin board where family members can see their children's work.

REFERENCES

Bell, Beverley. 1981. Animal, plant, living: Notes for teachers learning in science project. Working Paper No. 30.

Bell, Beverley, and Miles Barker. 1982. Towards a scientific concept of "Animal." *Journal of Biological Education* 16 (3): 197–200.

Osborne, Roger, and Peter Freyberg. 1985. *Learning in science: The implications of children's science.* Portsmouth, N.H.: Heinemann Educational Books.

ISSUE: *I worry that when we go outside, my children will just want to run around and play.*

RESPONSE: Naturally, children want to play, and some will have more difficulty focusing than others. Before each outdoor exploration, try reviewing the difference between going outside to play and acting as young naturalists. Model the young naturalists' behaviors you expect children to practice, such as looking closely and carefully at plants. Also, bring other adults to work alongside of you and engage with the naturalists. Similarly, if you can, bring out one small group of children at a time so you can focus on them.

ISSUE: *I don't have time to devote to observing children.*

RESPONSE: Many teachers struggle to find time to observe children. Some teachers keep pads of sticky notes and pens around the classroom so they can quickly scribble down a few words to remind them of important happenings. Other teachers divide up the group and observe specific children on specific days. A periodic review of your notes will provide the information you need to guide the children's inquiry.

Families and teachers can work together to support children's science learning in a variety of ways. One of the most powerful ways to partner is for family members to come into the classroom for the following:

- Share experiences or expertise

- Assist with small group explorations

- Provide guidance when children explore outdoors, helping them focus and observe more closely

open exploration

Step 1: Introduce Children to Discovering Nature

Three- to five-year-olds bring a natural curiosity and a sense of wonder to the world of living things. Some children in your class may have had many opportunities to explore and wonder. Others may have had few chances to really look closely at the animals they find underground or on a nearby leaf—or the plants that are poking up through the sidewalk. These initial explorations will provide children with common experiences as they observe and describe the living things in their immediate environment. Repeated outdoor explorations offer children opportunities to learn that there are many living things they can observe and wonder about.

CORE EXPERIENCES

- ☐ Observe plants and animals.
- ☐ Record and describe findings.

PREPARATION

- ☐ If you created a compost heap or you put out bug boards, see if they have attracted animals for children to observe.
- ☐ Do a safety check of the outdoor area where children will be exploring. Look for broken glass, poison ivy, and other potential dangers. See p. 121 for safety guidelines.
- ☐ Display books about local animals and plants around the room.
- ☐ Hang posters of local trees, animals, and plants.

□ Read the section on science teaching (pp. 115–119) for information about young children's inquiry and for strategies you can use to engage children in the exploration.

SCHEDULE

Set the schedule for the duration of a week, or until all children have participated in the following:

□ 30 minutes for outdoor exploration, two or three times during the week

□ 5–10 minutes for a meeting with the whole class before each outdoor exploration

□ 5–10 minutes for reflection with small groups after each outdoor exploration

□ 5–10 minutes for discussion with the whole group

MATERIALS

□ 6 clipboards with paper

□ Markers

□ Camera, if possible

□ Copies of the observation record form (p. 143) and the document annotation form (p. 144)

□ Charts labeled "What We Might See Outside" and "What We Found Outside"

FAMILY CONNECTION

□ Send home a note that introduces the "Discovering Nature" study and that suggests ways families might help. (See p. 131 for sample letter.)

□ Schedule and plan an evening when parents and other family members can meet in the classroom to talk about ways you can work together to support the study in and out of school.

TEACHING PLAN

ENGAGE

Lead a discussion with a large group, lasting five to ten minutes, before children's first outdoor exploration.

Discuss what children know about plants and animals.

When you start the exploration, gather the children together in a circle to discuss their prior experiences with plants and animals. Sample initial questions might include the following:

- *Tell us about an animal you have seen outside.*
  - *What did it look like?*

---

terrarium

ISSUE: *My children have a hard time sitting through discussions. What can I do?*

RESPONSE: Teachers find they are able to build children's interest in science talks by beginning with short meetings lasting four or five minutes. They also suggest engaging the children with an object, photograph, or drawing to focus the talk.

EXAMPLE:

WHAT WE MIGHT SEE OUTSIDE

cat	Shantay
Squirrel	Emily
Tiger	Brian
Flowers	Danny
Tree	Jorge

— *What was it doing?*
— *Where did you see it?*

- *Tell us about a plant you have seen outside.*
  — *What did it look like?*
  — *Where did you find it?*
  — *What did you notice about it?*

Ask follow-up questions, and invite other children to participate:

- *Kelly, do the birds you've seen always stay on the branch?*
- *Where do you think the birds go?*
- *Jose, have you seen birds like Kelly has?*

Share your excitement about becoming naturalists.

- Tell children that naturalists are people who study nature by looking carefully at plants and animals and finding out lots of things about them.
- Bring a houseplant, a live bug, or other small animal to the group and demonstrate looking at it closely, being gentle with it, and describing its shape, size, and parts.
- Ask children to think about what plants and animals they might see when they go outside and where they might find them. Write their predictions, using words and pictures, on a chart labeled "What We Might See Outside." Identify children's predictions with their names.

If children's responses seem unrealistic, you don't need to correct them. They will begin to gather firsthand evidence of their theories about living things when they explore outdoors.

Discuss how to be good naturalists.

- Stay safe (such as what can be touched, what should be avoided)
- Keep animals and plants safe
- Look very carefully at what they find

Tell children that they will be observing plants and animals in their natural environments outdoors; they will *not* bring indoors what they find. Assign no more than four children to each adult for the outdoor exploration.

EXPLORE

Take children on outdoor explorations for thirty minutes, two or three times during the week.

Encourage children to look outdoors for plants and animals.

Help children be naturalists by saying the following:

- *Where will you look for animals?*
- *Look at that red leaf you found. Which tree do you think it came from?*

EXAMPLE: This teacher was careful to include images as well as children's words.

Our Young Naturalist Rules

Trowels are for digging ⟁

Don't go near the swings

Look carefully ô͡ô

Touch carefully ✋

ISSUE: *Some children are more interested in playing than in exploring.*

RESPONSE: It is hard to know what to do when some children are more interested in playing than in exploring. Not all children need to be engaged in the science every time you go out, so letting some play is not a problem. The enthusiasm you and the explorers show for your work may draw in some others. You might also partner a child who is excited about the exploration with a child who is less engaged.

Also, model being a naturalist by doing some of the following:

- Turn over rocks and logs, and look for animals.
- Wonder aloud if you will see bugs or worms in the same places you found them before.
- Look closely at plants and comment on interesting features or how they have changed since the last time you were outdoors. Ask children what other changes they notice in the plants around them.
- Compare one plant to another, or one bug to another. Invite children to compare two plants or two animals.

Help children describe what they notice.

Encourage children to share what they found and where by using questions and comments such as these:

- *Tell me about what you found.*
- *What does it look like (such as shape, color, size, and so on)?*
- *How does it feel (such as slimy, smooth, bumpy, sticky, rough, and so on)?*
- *Where did you find it (such as over, under, beside, and so on)?*
- *Why do you think it was there?*

Show children the clipboards and markers, and invite them to draw a plant or animal in which they are interested.

Observe and document exploration.

As children explore, record their observations and ideas. You might do some of the following:

- Take photographs and/or make sketches of the plants and animals children notice and observe.
- Write down the questions children ask and the pieces of the conversations they have that relate to their role as naturalists.
- Use the observation forms to record what children say and do.

Later, use the document annotation forms to provide details about the photos and conversations. You will need this information to assess children's science learning. (See "Observation and Assessment" on p. 119.)

REFLECT

Discuss children's outdoor observations with small groups for five to ten minutes, and then again, after all children have been outdoors and have participated in a small group discussion, with the whole group for five to ten minutes.

Conduct science talks in small groups.

As soon as possible after each outdoor exploration, sit with small groups of children. Ask them to share their observations of plants and

---

TEACHER NOTE: Sonia has always been excited about plants and animals. But I just didn't have a clue about how she would go outside and explore in her wheelchair. It was her mom's idea to get a wedge. So now Sonia is one of my most eager naturalists. Supported by her wedge, she looks for ants, beetles, and pill bugs and talks to her classmates about what she sees and about what she might find next.

EXAMPLE: This teacher helps children compare two different kinds of plants.

> **Teacher:** *Maria's tall grass sure looks different from the dandelions Jamie found.*
>
> **Jamie:** *Mine has flowers.*
>
> **Teacher:** *The dandelion has two yellow flowers, and the tall grass doesn't have any flowers. How else are they different?*
>
> **Maria:** *Mine is skinny.*
>
> **Teacher:** *You're right. The tall grass is very thin.*

EXAMPLE: By including pictures and children's own words, you will help them remember their work.

> What We Found Outside
>
> Robin found ants ✳
>
> Karen found worms 〜
>
> José found a plant in a crack 🌱

animals, encouraging them to describe sizes, shapes, colors, and parts, and to use words to describe position and order. You might say something such as the following:

- *Tell us about a plant or animal you saw.*
- *What did you notice about its leaves, flowers, trunk, and so on?*
- *Tell us where you found it. Was it next to the log or under it?*

As you listen to children, you might also do the following:

- Make simple drawings of what each child describes, labeling them with the descriptive words the children use.
- Begin a chart titled "What We Found Outside," and continue to add to it as children make new observations.

Conduct a science talk with a large group.

Bring your whole group together in a circle. Invite children to talk about their early experiences as naturalists. Initiate a conversation with comments and questions such as the following:

- *Describe a plant or animal you saw.*
- *Where did you find it?*
- *Who else found things living in the dirt? What did they look like? How were they different from one another? How were they alike?*

Add to the "What We Found Outside" chart by recording children's observations in drawings and words.

Use the science talk for the following:

- Share a photograph or sketch of a plant or animal children observed outdoors.
- Invite a child to share a drawing of the plant or animal she observed outdoors.
- Ask children to help you make a list of everything they found under rocks or logs.
- Wonder with children about why they have been finding bugs under rocks and logs rather than sitting on sidewalks.
- Invite children to move like one of the animals they saw outdoors. Then talk with children about how the animals' movements are similar and how they are different.

At the end of the large group science talk, summarize what children have shared. For example: "Two of you noticed that the milkweed plants have green pods on them, and three of you said you liked watching the ants climb in and out of their holes. I wonder what you'll notice the next time we go out!"

EXAMPLE: An important science inquiry skill is communicating observations and ideas. In this example, the teacher asks children to use their bodies to show how different animals move. She then asks children to reflect on their observations by comparing how worms and centipedes move.

Teacher: *Jasmine moved like a worm, and Marcus moved like a centipede. What difference did you see in the way the worm moved and the way the centipede moved?*

Elsa: *Marcus was crawling.*

Teacher: *You're right. Marcus was crawling on his hands and knees. What about Jasmine? How was she moving?*

Sam: *On her belly!*

Yvonne: *Like a snake.*

Teacher: *Jasmine's worm was moving with her belly on the floor, and Marcus's centipede used its arms and legs to crawl along. Have you seen arms and legs on centipedes?*

REMINDERS

- Engaging children in outdoor explorations is central to discovering nature. Be sure that children continue to have opportunities to explore the outdoors for at least thirty minutes, two or three times a week, either as a large group, or in small groups if extra adult help is available. See step 4 of open exploration for guidance. Once a week, conduct a large group discussion or science talk about children's explorations. See teacher's role (p. 115) for strategies for facilitating science talks.

- Bring children outdoors to make monthly tree or bush observations. See step 4 (p. 72) of "Focused Exploration: Plants."

Step 2: Observing Living Things in an Indoor Terrarium

A mini-indoor environment will intrigue some children. Those who were actively engaged outdoors may make connections between what they see there and what they see in the terrarium. Others may find the terrarium a safe place to begin. In either case, the indoor environment will provide opportunities for children to look more closely at the characteristics and needs of their living visitors, while raising new questions.

CORE EXPERIENCES

☐ Observe and reflect on living things in the terrarium.

☐ Connect the observations made outdoors to what can be seen in the terrarium.

PREPARATION

☐ Construct a terrarium using plants and animals from the local outdoor environment. See pp. 123–125.

☐ Display, near the terrarium, books and posters about the animals and plants living there.

☐ Display the drawings that teachers or children made outdoors.

SCHEDULE

Set the schedule for the week, or until all children have participated in the following:

☐ 5–10 minutes for meeting to introduce the terrarium

☐ 45 minutes or more for choice time, four or five days during the week (Children will observe the terrarium during this time.)

☐ 5–10 minutes for reflection after each choice time

MATERIALS

☐ 6 clipboards with paper

☐ Markers

☐ Camera, if possible

☐ Copies of the observation record form (p. 143) and the document annotation form (p. 144)

☐ Chart labeled "What We Noticed in Our Terrarium"

FAMILY CONNECTION

☐ Send home notes periodically, detailing what children are doing and learning.

☐ Encourage family members to work with you in the classroom. Prepare a brief explanation of what they might do to facilitate children's exploration of the terrarium and some guidelines.

☐ Plan and host an afternoon workshop for families. Have them make plant terrariums to bring home.

TEACHING PLAN

ENGAGE

Present the terrarium in a five- to ten-minute meeting with the whole group.

Introduce the terrarium.

Gather the whole group together in a circle. Facilitate a conversation about children's prior experiences with terrariums by asking questions such as the following:

- *Do you have plants or animals at home?*
- *Where do they live? Who takes care of them? What do they need?*
- *Have you ever seen a terrarium before? What was in it?*
- *Who took care of the terrarium? What did they do?*

Show the terrarium to the whole group. Explain that the terrarium is a place for plants and animals to live indoors. Tell children they will be naturalists as they observe the plants and animals in the terrarium.

Use the terrarium to engage children in conversation about what they see:

- *What do you see? What do you notice about it?*
- *What else do you think is in here?*

Talk about maintaining the terrarium.

Establish the steps you and the children will need to follow to maintain the terrarium and to keep the plants and animals healthy and safe. Ask questions that focus on how to care for living things:

- *What do you need to stay healthy?*
- *What do you think the plants and animals in the terrarium need in order to live?*
- *What do you think we'll need to do to keep the plants and animals healthy?*

Explain that while they may look, children will not open the terrarium or handle the living things inside. Post a list of ways you will keep the plants and animals healthy near the terrarium table, using words and pictures.

Introduce chart.

Before transitioning to choice time, show children the chart titled "What We Noticed in Our Terrarium." Tell children they will use this

---

EXAMPLE:

KEEPING LIVING THINGS HEALTHY

* Keep plants wet but not too wet.

* Keep the terrarium out of the sun.

* Keep the terrarium closed.

Most of the children will not be able to read the charts. But you can refer to them regularly, pointing out key words such as *terrarium*. Some children will eventually learn to identify these words.

chart to record what they see, using words and pictures, when they're observing the plants and animals in the terrarium. Remind children that they will all have opportunities to look closely at the plants and animals in the terrarium—sometimes with you at the table, and sometimes as a small group of young naturalists on their own.

EXPLORE

Encourage children to observe plants and animals in the terrarium during choice time until all children have had a chance to make more than one observation.

Invite children to observe the terrarium with you.

As you sit with children, encourage them to describe what they notice about the plants and animals in the terrarium by asking questions such as the following:

- *What can you see? Tell me about it.*

- *Is that something you have seen outside? Where? Under a leaf? In the dirt?*

- *How many leaves does it have?*

- *I wonder what it needs to live.*

Refer to the drawings and photos from the outdoor explorations that you posted. Use them to help children compare their outdoor and indoor observations of plants and animals. You might ask the following: "Do you think the worm in our terrarium is longer than the one we found outside under the leaves? How might we find out?"

Add responses to the chart titled "What We Noticed in Our Terrarium."

Observe and document children's terrarium explorations.

As children observe, record their observations, questions, and ideas. You might do the following:

- Take photographs and/or make sketches of the plants and animals that children notice and observe.

- Write down children's questions and the snippets of their conversations that relate to their role as naturalists.

- Use the observation forms to record what children say and do.

For example, this annotation reveals children's interests in worm behavior. The teacher can use this information to help children pursue their interests.

DOCUMENT ANNOTATION

Child(ren): _Kendra, Alex_   Date: _Sept. 5_

Context/Setting: _Kendra and Alex had seen a worm in the terrarium yesterday, but couldn't_
find it. They talked about where it went.

Science Concepts Explored/Evidence: _A worm's Needs ("It wants to be in the dirt"),_
it's characteristics ("It digs"), and habitat (they seemed to agree that it wasn't good
for the worm to leave the dirt)

ISSUE: *I know it's important to spend time with children during choice time, but I'm pulled in so many directions.*

RESPONSE: Finding time to sit with children during choice time can be a challenge. Some teachers have had success planning activities where most of the children play independently in different areas of the room, so they can focus their attention on the children doing science. They also ask volunteers to help other children.

EXAMPLE: This teacher chose to work with only three children at a time so they would all be able to see the same things, then talk about what they had observed.

Later, use the document annotation forms to provide details about the photos and conversations. Use this information to assess children's science learning. (See "Observation and Assessment" on p. 119.)

REFLECT

Share and discuss observations of terrarium during a science talk, lasting five to ten minutes, with the whole group.

Conduct a science talk with a large group.

Gather your group together in a circle to share their terrarium observations. Share your documentation panel and ask questions such as these to focus the discussion:

- *What plants/animals do you look at?*
- *What did you notice about that plant/animal?*
- *What do you wonder about the plant/animal?*

Record children's responses, using words and pictures, on the chart labeled "What We Noticed in Our Terrarium."

MAKE CONNECTIONS

Help children make connections between their outdoor and indoor explorations by asking questions such as the following:

- *How are the plants/animals in our terrarium like the ones we see outdoors? How are they different?*
- *We take care of the plants and animals in our terrarium. How do the plants and animals that live outdoors stay healthy and alive?*

> **TEACHER NOTE:** Children have been busy observing and caring for the plants and animals in their indoor terrarium. And when we go outdoors to look at living things in their natural environments, they are really beginning to see the outdoors as a place where plants and animals must meet their own needs.

Step 3: Teach Children How to Use Naturalist Tools

Many of the children's observations will be through direct sensory experience. But children can also use naturalist tools (such as hand lenses, penlights, and trowels) to extend their ability to see and focus on details that they may otherwise have missed. Penlights, for example, make it possible for children to see plants and animals that live in dark places (under rocks or leaves). Children can use trowels to carefully dig up plants. While tools are useful, learning how to use them properly and safely takes time and practice. As children learn to use these tools, they will become better observers of the plants and animals around them.

CORE EXPERIENCES

☐ Learn to use hand lenses, penlights, trowels, and tongue depressors.

Preparation

Schedule

Set schedule for the week, or until all children have participated in the following:

☐ 5–10 minutes for a meeting to introduce the tools

☐ 45 minutes or more for choice time, for four or five days or until all children have been able to practice using the tools indoors and outdoors

Materials

☐ 6 each: hand lenses, penlights, trowels, and tongue depressors

☐ Paper with print, photographs, paintings, rocks, shells, leaves, or feathers

☐ Field guides with pictures of some of the plants and animals that are in the terrarium (See "Books and Videos" on p. 130 for suggestions.)

Teaching Plan

Engage

Introduce tools in a meeting with the whole group that lasts five to ten minutes.

Introduce tools.

Gather your whole group together. Show children a hand lens or a penlight and lead a discussion about their prior experiences with these tools by asking questions such as the following:

- *What do you think this is?*

- *What do you think it does? How do you know? Why do you think so?*

- *Have you ever seen/used one of these hand lenses/penlights before?*

- *If you have used one, what did you look at? What did it help you notice? How did you use it?*

- *If you have seen someone else use one, what was it being used for?*

- *How do you think we can use it as naturalists?*

Prepare for small group work.

Show children some of the objects you've collected for them to look at closely with the tools.

- Tell them that these objects will be at a small table, along with the penlights and hand lenses, so they can practice using the naturalist tools.

- Tell them that they will also be able to practice using the tools to look more closely at the plants and animals in the terrarium.

EXPLORE INDOORS

Guide children as they use hand lenses and penlights during choice times, until all interested children have had opportunities to practice using both tools.

Support children as they learn to use the hand lenses indoors.

As you sit with a small group of children during choice time, invite them to use the hand lenses to look closely at the different objects you've collected. If they need your help using the hand lenses, show them how by looking at something such as your finger or a picture. Then help each child position the lens until it magnifies the image.

Invite children to use penlights, hand lenses, and field guides to look more closely at the plants and animals in the terrarium.

- Take the top off the terrarium and invite two children at a time to use the hand lenses and penlights to observe the plants and animals.

- Engage interested children in conversation by asking them what they like looking at and what they notice about it.

- Show children illustrations in a field guide of the plants and animals they're observing. Invite them to compare what they're seeing to these illustrations. Ask questions such as the following: Does the dandelion leaf you're looking at look like the one in the book? How? or Why not?

EXPLORE OUTDOORS

Guide children who use the naturalist tools. (Interested children have had opportunities to practice using trowels, hand lenses, and penlights.)

Introduce the trowels and tongue depressors.

During your next outdoor exploration, sit with your small group and introduce children to the trowels and tongue depressors. Encourage them to share their experiences with equipment by asking questions such as the following:

- *What do you think this is for?*

- *When have you used a trowel?*

- *How did you use it? What did you find?*

- *How can we as naturalists use it?*

- *How might we carry and dig with them safely?*

Also, introduce the tongue depressors, which will be used as science probes to pick up and move small animals without hurting them.

TEACHER NOTE: I never thought Jeremy would be able to use the hand lens. He just has so little muscle control. I did put a bigger grip on the hand lens, but he still had trouble. It was Tanya—a four-year-old—who came up with the perfect solution. She now holds the hand lens steady for Jeremy, so he can really look closely at the plants and animals he's studying.

EXAMPLE: At first, the kids used the tools as props for their dramatic play. But now I'm really working on helping kids use the hand lenses correctly. This time, I knew that Latisha got it right when she started pointing out details that she had never noticed before.

ISSUE: *We have so many tools. It's hard to keep them organized. How will we ever transport them when we go outside?*

RESPONSE: One teacher transformed an old wagon into a mobile naturalist station. She said it was perfect for moving the hand lenses, penlights, and digging and collecting equipment, as well as all the clipboards, paper, and writing utensils.

Encourage children to use the trowels, science probes, hand lenses, penlights, and field guides.

Ask children to use the trowels to carefully dig up plants. Encourage children to use the hand lenses and penlights to look closely at plants and animals. Talk to children about how they are using the tools and about what they observe. You might ask the following questions:

- *What did you find when you used the penlight?*

- *What new things do you notice about the leaf when you use the hand lens?*

Show children illustrations in a field guide of the plants and animals they're observing. Invite them to compare what they're seeing to these illustrations: Do you think this caterpillar looks like the one you're watching? How? or Why not?

REMINDER

Conduct a large group discussion or "science talk" about children's explorations once a week.

Step 4: Ongoing Explorations and Reflections

By continuing to explore the outdoors with hand lenses, penlights, and digging tools, as well as observing the terrarium, children will begin to look more closely around them at plants and animals and their habitats. Through these ongoing experiences, children will develop important ideas and raise interesting questions about living things, while building the foundation they need for future, more focused explorations.

Core Experiences

- ☐ Observe plants and animals indoors and outdoors.
- ☐ Record and describe findings.

Preparation

- ☐ Continue safety checks. Look for broken glass, poison ivy, and other dangerous items in the area where children will be exploring.
- ☐ Display drawings that you (at children's eye level) and children make during the outdoor explorations.
- ☐ Refer again to the section on observation and assessment (p. 119) for strategies and tools you can use to capture children's engagement and their science understandings.

Schedule

- ☐ 30 minutes for outdoor exploration, two or three times a week
- ☐ 5–10 minutes for a meeting before each outdoor exploration
- ☐ 5–10 minutes for reflection with children after each outdoor exploration

☐ 45 minutes or more for choice time, four or five days a week
(Children will be able to observe the terrarium during this time.)

☐ 5–10 minutes for a science talk each week

MATERIALS

☐ 6 naturalist kits: a cloth bag containing a trowel, tongue depressors, hand lens, and penlight

☐ 6 clipboards with paper

☐ Markers

☐ Field guide of local plants and small animals

☐ Camera, if possible

☐ Copies of the observation record form (p. 143) and the document annotation form (p. 144)

FAMILY CONNECTION

☐ Send home notes that suggest families sign-up to borrow the naturalists' tools over the weekend.

☐ Encourage family members to explore the local parks for living things with their children. Send home directions to local parks and a description of each one's unique features.

TEACHING PLAN

ENGAGE

Make connections from one exploration to the next during a five- to ten-minute meeting with the whole group before each indoor or outdoor exploration.

Discuss what children know.

Gather the children together and help them think about their previous indoor and outdoor explorations. You might share a photo, a child's drawing, or an illustration of a plant or animal children observed. Help them reflect on a previous exploration by asking some of the following questions:

- *When we were outdoors last time, some of you saw a plant like this. Can you tell me about it? Where was it? Were there others like it?*

- *This is a picture of a pill bug. Who noticed a pill bug in the terrarium yesterday? Where was it? What was it doing?*

Help children make predictions.

Help children predict what they might observe during this upcoming observation by asking some of these questions:

- *Here's a picture we took of a dandelion. When we go outdoors and look at the dandelion plant again, do you think it will look the same as it did last week? In what way? How might it look different?*

EXAMPLE: I asked LaBreshia to show her spider drawing at circle time. She looked so proud as she held her picture up. And she was able to use the picture to describe what the spider looked like and how she found it.

- *Yesterday I drew a picture of the ant Noah noticed in the terrarium. Noah, do you think we'll see the ant again today? Where might we see it? What else might we see?*

Show children a naturalist kit. Tell them that the kits will be available outdoors and indoors for their use. Ask children how they might use the naturalists' tools to help them find changes outdoors or in the terrarium.

Explore

Explore outdoors and at the indoor terrarium for thirty minutes, two or three times during each of these two weeks, or until children are ready for a focused exploration of plants.

Encourage children to continue exploring and observing.

When children explore plants and animals outdoors and in the terrarium, encourage them to use their senses and their naturalist tools to find and observe living things. Make observations and ask questions such as the following:

- *I wonder what we'll find today under this rock. Remember yesterday when we saw some worms?*
- *What can you see when you use the penlight?*

Compare illustrations from field guides to the plants and animals they explore. Ask: How are they alike? How are they different?

Remind children that you brought clipboards, paper, and markers so they can draw or write about what they see. Help them follow up on some of their earlier ideas. For example, if children had been wondering if all leaves have stems, remind them of their question. Then invite them to look at different kinds of leaves to see if they have stems.

You can also ask the following questions:

- *Who remembers where we found a lot of pointy leaves last time?*
- *Jon, are any of those beetles you found before under the board today?*

Share Observations and Ideas

Engage children in conversation about what they notice.

Encourage children to describe what they see, hear, smell, and feel by asking some of these questions:

- *What do you see? Tell me about it.*
- *What does it look like (shape, size, color, and so on)?*
- *How is it moving? Show me with your body.*

Help children describe the places where they find interesting plants and animals, as well as the things they wonder about:

- *Are you finding things in the same places each time?*
- *Why do you think that is?*

Issue: *The children want to bring the creatures indoors so that others can see what they've discovered.*

Response: In order to make it easier for children to leave the creatures outdoors, one teacher had a parade at the end of each outdoor exploration. All the children sat down in a line. Those who had something to share would walk down the line, showing and describing what they had discovered. After the parade, the teacher reminded the children that the creatures needed to be returned to their outdoor homes.

Teacher note: School was a real struggle for Brent at the beginning. He hit kids. He'd take their things. At first, I wasn't sure how he would ever be able to participate in "Discovering Nature." But I've been working really hard, helping him to get ready. We've been reading books about the needs of plants and animals. We talk a lot about how to care for them. And then we explore together, and each time I tell him what is going to happen, what he can do. And he's making progress! I was so thrilled to see Brent with Sean observing snails. They were both so engaged, looking at snails through the magnifying glass, handling the snails really gently, and talking about what it felt like when the snails walked up their arms.

Observe and document children's continuing exploration.

Record the plants and animals that capture children's interest and how children use naturalist tools to extend their senses. You might do the following:

- Photograph and/or make sketches of the plants and animals children notice and observe.

- Jot down snippets of children's conversations or words they use to describe what they see or how they are using the naturalist tools.

- Use the observation forms to record what children say and do.

Use the document annotation forms to provide details about photos, conversations, or children's work samples. You will use this information, along with the records you've been collecting, for your upcoming science talks. This information will also help you decide when to initiate a focused exploration of plants or animals (pp. 38–39).

Create a documentation panel.

Use your photographs, sketches, and notes about children's experiences, observations, and ideas to create a documentation panel. See guidelines for creating documentation panels on p. 142. The panel can be used during science talks.

REFLECT

Share and discuss observations with small groups of interested naturalists for five to ten minutes, two or three times each week, and in a science talk with the whole group for five to ten minutes, once a week.

Conduct small group science talks.

Following each outdoor or indoor exploration, sit with a few of the explorers and help them to share their observations and reflect on their ideas. You might do the following:

- Ask children what they liked about being naturalists.

- Invite each child to share their drawings or describe a plant or animal that interested them.

- Encourage children to demonstrate what they have observed: Can you show us how the worm moved? How did the dandelion move in the wind?

- Ask them to share their ideas about how the animals they saw survive, or what will happen to the dandelion.

Write down children's observations and ideas. Use your notes to focus the upcoming science talk.

Look at books.

Look at field guides and reference books with small groups of children, and help them find pictures of plants and animals they have

---

TEACHER NOTE: Outside, Ronnie found a few worms under a piece of slate, and then found more in a hole that he dug in the dirt. I asked him why he thought there were worms in both places but he didn't answer. He seems very interested in worms so this is a question I'll have to come back to when he's ready. I decided to take a photo of him so I could sit with him later, discuss the photos, and find out more about what he thinks.

ISSUE: *How will I know when children are ready to move from open exploration to focused exploration?*

RESPONSE: When children begin to focus on a particular plant or animal or begin to pursue a question (how an animal moves, how a plant grows), they may be ready for more focused explorations. (See "Transition from Open Exploration to Focused Exploration," p. 38, for more clues. Also see "Observation and Assessment" on p. 119 to help you assess if children are ready.)

seen in the terrarium or outdoors. Talk about the pictures. You might ask questions like these:

- *Did anyone see one of these?*
- *How does the plant on this page look like the one you found this morning?*
- *Did the worm you were looking at have lines on its body like this one?*

Ask children if any of them would like to share a field guide picture of a plant or animal they saw outside or in the terrarium with the group during a science talk.

Conduct a large group science talk.

Gather your whole group together once a week, and initiate a science talk by using one of the following strategies:

- Share your documentation panel. (*Where did you find the most bugs? Why do you think the bugs were there?*)
- Share a photograph of children looking closely at a plant or animal. (*Tell me about what you were doing in this photograph.*)
- Share a child's drawing of a plant or animal. (*Tell me about a plant or animal you observed. What did it look like?*)
- Share a story from the observational notes of the naturalists' exploration. (*Beth said that she found lots of pill bugs under a log. Can you tell us about them, Beth?*)

Probe children's thought process with follow-up questions such as these:

- *What new thing did you notice when you used the hand lens or the penlight?*
- *What was your favorite thing to look at? Why?*

Record children's descriptions on the chart labeled "What We Found Outside," and summarize findings after you've read the chart aloud to the children. For example: You've found lots of anthills and you like digging for worms. The plants you like best are the ones with the seeds that blow through the air—dandelions and milkweeds.

✓ Transition from Open Exploration to Focused Exploration

When children are engaged in open exploration, they notice, wonder, and ask general questions about the plants and animals they see outdoors and in the classroom terrarium. Children's questions are expressed in actions and words. For example, during open exploration a child may look under a rock to see what he can find. Or a child might say, "Let's go by the swings to see if there are more dandelions."

During a focused exploration, children plan an investigation that focuses on a question that is central to their particular interest. They

EXAMPLE: This teacher keeps the discussion focused on where things are found. Later, she can help children find some patterns.

> **Teacher:** *What did you find outside?*
>
> **Ann:** *A spider.*
>
> **Teacher:** *Yes, you did. Where did you find it? (The teacher shows her the clipboard with a list of everything the children found.)*
>
> **Ann:** *In the grass.*
>
> **Mira:** *I found an ant and I found more ants . . . and more.*
>
> **Teacher:** *So you found a lot of ants. Where did you find them?*
>
> **Mira:** *In the grass. They were going to the house. They were sleeping because they want to sleep and then they tired.*

TEACHER NOTE: I found some great field guides in a used bookstore. Kids love to compare the pictures in the field guides to the plants and animals they're observing. I've noticed, too, that when children use field guides as references, they begin to develop concepts of the purpose of print, even if they can't read the words yet.

TEACHER NOTE: For weeks, children have been really interested in worms. They look for worms in the dirt and under logs. They talk about what they notice, not only during our science talks, but at the lunch table too. Some kids are beginning to ask questions such as, "How do worms move? How do they get under the ground? How do they eat?" Some kids have been drawing pictures of worms too. So, I'm thinking it might be a good time to begin a more focused study of worms.

make new observations and record and represent their experiences. They reflect on their actions and look for patterns and relationships. Oftentimes these reflections lead them to ask new questions. These experiences can also lead to the formulation of new understandings or theories based on the evidence they have gathered.

When children begin to focus their observations and ask specific questions about plants or animals, they may be ready for focused exploration. Samples of more focused questions include the following: Will I find snails on the wall again today? Do snails like to be on rocks more than on other places? How does a snail move? What do worms eat? What will happen if we plant this acorn?

If most of your children have been engaged in observing plants and animals a number of times over the past few weeks, many of them may have developed a particular interest. There are some signs to look for to determine which children might like to pursue a more focused question or exploration. These signs include the following:

- Showing interest in observing a single animal or plant from one day to the next (For example, children return to look under a rotting log for pill bugs, or they notice the growing number of dandelions that have gone to seed, or they check the top of the terrarium to find snails.)

- Wondering about a particular aspect or characteristic of a living thing (such as how it moves, how quickly it grows, or what it eats)

- Looking in books to find photos or information about plants or animals they observed outdoors or in the terrarium

Focused exploration includes two different studies. The plant study focuses on plants' growth and development, the interrelatedness of their different parts, their needs, and their life cycle. This study relies on regular indoor and outdoor explorations as well as monthly observations of a tree or bush.

The animal study focuses on animals' body parts and their functions, their behaviors and needs, and their life cycles. The animal study relies on regular explorations of animals in the indoor terrarium and outdoors in their natural habitats.

You may notice that some of your children will remain engaged in open exploration and might want to continue to explore broadly, which is fine. They can continue with open exploration while others shift to focused exploration. Participating in the group discussions, observing, and listening to the children who are studying particular plants and animals more closely will help those still in open exploration become interested in more focused questions.

focused exploration: plants

Children have looked for plants in their outdoor environment and in the class terrarium. Now it's time to look more closely at all kinds of plants—trees, bushes, houseplants, sprouted seeds, and so on—and to begin to see them as living things that have some common structures and needs. Also, plants can grow and change over time. Some changes, particularly in many of the indoor plants, will be observable quickly. Other changes, particularly in trees and other outdoor plants, will occur over much longer time periods. By creating an indoor world of plants, inviting children to "get to know" a number of different outdoor plants as they change from season to season, and comparing plants indoors to those outdoors, you tap into children's natural sense of wonder while deepening their understanding of the characteristics of living things.

This focused exploration consists of two strands: one indoors and one outdoors. Indoors you will need to begin a number of plants from seeds, cuttings, and bulbs. And you will need to continue to start plants every week or two in order for your room to have a variety of plants in different stages of development for children to observe over a number of weeks. Consider where in the classroom these plants could be placed. The ideal spot would be sunny and away from radiators or drafty windows. The more light and even warmth available, the better chance your plants will have of surviving. "Essential Information" (p. 121) has directions for starting and caring for plants as well as making and caring for a terrarium.

While children explore indoor plants, you will continue the outdoor exploration. Arrange for the class to continue to go outdoors as often as possible, ideally at least once each week to observe all kinds of outdoor plants and then make comparisons to the plants that are developing indoors. You will also go out to observe one tree or bush each month over the course of the year to gain more experience with growth and change over a long period of time.

Although plants are often associated with springtime, the fall is the ideal time to begin this exploration. The earlier plants are started, the more opportunities children will have to see growth and change over time. Children will be able to make eight or nine monthly tree observations if they are started as soon as the school year begins. Looking at plants in all seasons reinforces children's experiences with a life cycle. Also, many trees have interesting seeds and leaves that make dramatic changes in the fall.

Field trips to ponds, meadows, swamps, wet woods, or nature centers give children opportunities to observe and wonder about a variety of plants and habitats. Guest visitors can share their knowledge about local plants and their habitats, providing children with new information about plants, their needs, and the ways they adapt to their environments. The extension section (p. 107) has suggestions for field trips, guest visitors, and books.

See the section on science teaching (p. 115) for information about young children's inquiry and for strategies you can use to focus and deepen their experiences and thinking during the exploration.

Step 1: Growing Plants

Three- to five-year-olds love to plant seeds, bulbs, tubers, and cuttings, and they love to care for their plants. By trying a number of ways to begin new plants indoors, children will find that various plants look very different but have similar needs. Children will also encounter a number of ways to start new plants, such as from seeds, bulbs, cuttings, and so on.

CORE EXPERIENCES

- ☐ Share experiences growing plants.
- ☐ Start plants from seeds, cuttings, bulbs, or tubers.
- ☐ Reflect on plants' needs and plan for ways to meet those needs.
- ☐ Predict what the plants might look like as they grow.

PREPARATION

- ☐ Set up a plant center at a table that can accommodate a small group, near an empty, sunny, not-too-cool windowsill or another table.
- ☐ Display books about growing different kinds of plants around the classroom.
- ☐ Hang posters of different stages of a variety of growing plants around the classroom.

SCHEDULE

Set schedule for the next two weeks:

☐ 45–60 minutes for choice time, two or three times a week

☐ 5–10 minutes for a meeting before each choice time

☐ 10–15 minutes for a discussion with the whole group, once a week

MATERIALS

☐ Carrots and beets

☐ Bean seeds, radish seeds, and other seeds that haven't been treated with fungicide

☐ Garlic bulbs and flower bulbs

☐ Potato with eyes

☐ Cuttings from plants such as geraniums that root easily

☐ Seed tray

☐ Potting soil

☐ Plant mister

☐ Chart labeled "What We Know about Helping Plants Grow"

FAMILY CONNECTION

In your next newsletter, include a few paragraphs about the plants children have started and provide information about how they might start plants at home too. Invite family members who are gardeners to visit the classroom and share their gardening interests, tools, and/or experiences with the children.

TEACHING PLAN

ENGAGE

Introduce planting in a discussion with the whole group for five to ten minutes.

Share experiences.

Gather children together in a circle and invite them to share experiences they've had planting seeds, bulbs, tubers, and cuttings. Show them the materials you have at the plant center (seeds, cuttings, tubers, bulbs, seed tray, soil, plant mister) and ask the following questions:

- *I've brought in some things so we can grow plants in our classroom. Have you ever grown plants?*
- *How did you start them growing?*
- *What did you do to help them grow?*

Help children focus in on the materials by asking questions such as the following:

- *What can you tell me about this carrot? Do you think it can grow? What might we need to help it grow?*

- *Here is a bean seed. What might we need to make it grow?*

- Show children a garlic bulb and ask them, *"Have you seen something like this before? What do you think it can be?"*

Listen carefully to what children have to say, and record their comments in pictures and words on the chart labeled "What We Know about Helping Plants Grow." Accept their ideas, even if you feel they're incorrect. For example, a child may say that plants need dirt to grow, in which case you can say, "It does look like plants need dirt. I wonder if we'll ever see plants that don't need dirt to grow." Plan to post the chart near the plant center so you can add to or revise it throughout the exploration.

Discuss ways children can care for the growing plants.

Introduce children to their role as plant caregivers by showing them the water mister, small watering can, additional flower pots, and extra potting soil. Ask them to share experiences they've had with these tools by asking questions such as the following:

- *Have you ever seen anyone using this?*

- *What do you think it is?*

- *What were they doing with it?*

Help children think about how the tools can help them take care of their plants by asking questions such as the following:

- *Why will we need a water mister to take care of our plants?*

- *What about the watering can? How is it different from the mister?*

- *When do you think we'll need to use the bigger pots and extra potting soil? Why?*

EXPLORE

Start plants during choice time, until all interested children have participated.

Guide the planting.

- During choice times, sit with children at the plant center, and invite them to choose a seed, bulb, tuber, or cutting to plant. Ask them what they need to plant it and how to plant it. Even if their ideas are quite different from yours, let them try it out.

- If you think the child's method is not going to produce a growing plant, invite her to do another one, this time following your directions. If she is planting only seeds, suggest planting three or four of the same seed in the pot so she can be sure to have at least one healthy seedling. You'll be able to help her compare the two later after a few weeks.

TEACHER NOTE: Alba talked about her father's garden, complete with chili peppers, avocados, papayas, and special kinds of corn. I'm going to call her father to see if he can bring in some seeds and help us with our garden. I'm sure he'll have a lot to teach us about the kinds of plants that are grown in Mexico.

ISSUE: *My children have all kinds of crazy ideas about what makes plants grow. How will they possibly understand the real answers?*

RESPONSE: It is normal for young children, especially those who have had little to no real experience with plants, to have what seem to be unusual ideas. One goal of science for young children is to provide them with many opportunities to observe and reflect on real plants. Over time, their ideas about plants will be based more on direct observation and will be closer to the "real" answers.

TEACHER NOTE: Yesterday I took a small group of children to a nearby nursery. Children were intrigued. They looked at all the different plants. They watched the gardeners water the plants and tend to them. They asked gardeners questions about how the different plants grow. When we got back to the classroom, they were all so excited and couldn't wait to tell the others about their experiences. It was Nathaniel who renamed our plant center. He said that for now on we should call it our "plant nursery." So we made a new sign. And now all the kids are pretending to be gardeners. Dressed in their hats and aprons, they help "customers," while tending to their plants.

- Make sure children label their plants. They will be observing their plants' growth and development over the next few months and will want to remember which pot holds their seed, bulb, or cutting.

Invite children to describe and draw their planting experience.

- Invite children to describe and draw what the seeds, tubers, cuttings, and bulbs look like after they've been planted, or what they think the plants will look like after they've grown some.

- As they finish their drawings, ask children to tell you about them and ask, "What will your plant need to grow?" Write their words down next to their drawings.

- Later, use the document annotation forms to highlight what children's drawings and words reveal about their inquiry skills and their understanding of the characteristics and needs of living things.

Observe and document children's planting experiences.

An important aspect to look for is children's ideas about how their plants will grow, and what they will need to grow and stay healthy. Use the observation record forms to jot down the important parts of conversations you have with children about the following:

- How their plants will grow: What will their plants look like as they grow—in a week, in a month, and so on?

- What their plants need to grow and stay healthy

By keeping observation records, you can begin to see patterns in children's responses that can guide teaching. For instance, the teacher in this example might focus on asking children to explain the thinking behind their predictions by asking questions such as, "What makes you think that?"

ISSUE: *My kids think they should water the plants all the time, but that actually might kill them. What should I do?*

RESPONSE: It is hard to know how and when to intervene, but encouraging children to try out their own strategies for maintaining plants can contribute to their learning. Sometimes, in hopes of caring for plants, they can care too much. How you respond will depend on how many plants you have. If you have many, it will be fine for children to learn from experience that too much water can kill the plants. If you have only a few prized plants you might not wish to take that risk. Also, if you start several sets of plants, you can use some for experiments.

ISSUE: *Children who have trouble responding verbally get frustrated when I ask so many questions.*

RESPONSE: If your children are engaged, it is good to leave them to their work. When they are ready to share, you can provide opportunities for them to communicate in ways other than words. By drawing, pointing, and using their bodies, they can share their observations and ideas.

	OBSERVATION RECORD	
Teacher _Becky_		Date: _September 29_
Setting: _Plant table_		
Check one: ☐ Open Exploration ☒ Focused Exploration		
Check one: ☒ Plants ☐ Animals		
Step: _I_		

Children's Names	Seen and Heard
Jasmine	"It's gonna be a tree when I'm 10." (when planting a bean seed) "I water it every day."
Andrew	(Narcissus bulb) "It looks like a onion." When asked what will happen, says "I don't know."
Betty	(Bean plant) "Mine is going to be as big as a dinosaur."

If possible, take photos or make sketches of the seed trays, flower pots, and cuttings every few days so children can reflect on changes over time.

Create a documentation panel of children's planting experiences.

Use your photographs, sketches, and notes as well as children's work to create a documentation panel. (See p. 142 for suggestions.) This is a good time to let families know about children's new focus on growing plants. Include a statement about how children are using their observation skills to learn about plants' needs and development, and that they are planning an investigation to find out more about both.

REFLECT

Share planting experiences and discuss plants' needs in a science talk with the whole group for ten to fifteen minutes.

Have children reflect on their planting experiences.

Sit with children in a circle and help them remember what they planted. Bring some of the flower pots from the plant center to the circle, and ask questions such as the following:

- *What did you plant in the flower pot?*
- *What did it look like?*
- *What did you have to do to plant it?*

Talk about the plants' needs.

Help children reflect on the plants' needs by sharing the documentation panel you made and asking questions such as the following:

- *What do you think this seed (bulb, cutting, tuber) will need to grow?*
- *Do you think all of these growing plants will need the same things?*
- *What do you think the plants in our terrarium will need to grow?*
- *What do you think the plants that grow outdoors need to grow?*

Help children plan ways they can take care of their plants' needs by asking questions such as the following:

- *How can we make sure our plants get what they need?*
- *How will we know if they need more or less water?*
- *Who will be in charge of watering the plants?*
- *What are some good ways to water seeds? Seedlings? Big plants?*

Share ideas about the plants as they grow.

Help children think about what the seeds, bulbs, tubers, and cuttings might look like as they grow by sharing some of the drawings they made at the plant center and asking questions such as the following:

- *Tell us about your drawing.*
- *What did it look like when you planted it?*

These kinds of questions introduce children to the idea of making predictions. Initially, children will really be guessing, as a true prediction implies that children have some experience or evidence on which to base it. Over time, children will begin to use their experiences to make more accurate predictions.

REMINDERS

- Every week or two, help children begin a new set of plants, which will allow them to compare examples of bean, avocado, narcissus, and carrot plants, for example, at different stages of development. Of course, they can also start other kinds of plants throughout the year, adding them to the plant center.

- As children grow and care for their plants, be sure to bring children outdoors to make tree or bush observations once a month. See step 4 of "Focused Exploration: Plants" (p. 72).

- *What do you think it will look like when it grows?*

- *How big do you think it will be? Do you think it will ever have flowers? Why do you think that?*

- *How are some of these growing plants the same? How are they different?*

Step 2: Monitoring Plant Growth and Development

By now your children have experienced plants at many different stages, from germinating seeds to healthy houseplants to trees. By paying careful attention to caring for plants and keeping track of their progress over time—how they grow, how much they grow, when they produce flowers and perhaps seeds, even when they die—children will learn more about what plants need and about their life cycles.

CORE EXPERIENCES

- ☐ Care for plants.
- ☐ Observe plant growth and development.
- ☐ Measure and record changes.

PREPARATION

- ☐ Sprout seeds and grow plants in a plastic bottle, without soil, so children will be able to see developing roots. See "Growing and Caring for Plants" on pp. 127–129 for guidance.
- ☐ Prepare a display space for graphs and records of plants' growth and development.
- ☐ Plan to take children on a field trip to explore another habitat. See extensions on pp. 107–109 for guidance.

SCHEDULE

- ☐ 5–10 minutes for a meeting before each choice time or outdoor exploration
- ☐ 45–60 minutes for choice time to observe, measure, and record changes in plants
- ☐ 20–30 minutes for outdoor exploration, once or twice a week
- ☐ 10–15 minutes for a science talk, once a week

MATERIALS

- ☐ 6 hand lenses
- ☐ 6 of one kind of measuring tool: pieces of string, rulers, cloth measuring tapes, or paper strips
- ☐ 6 clipboards with paper

☐ Markers

☐ Camera, if possible

☐ Copies of the observation record form (p. 143) and the document annotation form (p. 144)

FAMILY CONNECTION

Invite families into the classroom one evening for a planting party. You might plant seeds that will grow into seedlings that can then be planted in a school garden, or families might take the plants home and observe development with their children. Ask community businesses to donate supplies.

TEACHING PLAN

ENGAGE

Introduce the plant growth and development to the whole group for five to ten minutes.

Talk about how plants grow.

Bring children together in a circle. Talk about changes they have noticed in the indoor plants they're growing. Show a plant, such as a bean plant, that has made obvious growth. Ask questions such as the following:

- *Do you remember how this plant looked when we first started it?*

- *How has it changed?*

As children talk about the changes they have noticed, record their descriptions in words and drawings on a chart. Then ask them what changes they think the plants will make over the next several weeks with a question such as, "Why do you think it will look like that after it's grown some more?"

Add their ideas to the chart.

Talk about tracking plant growth and development.

Tell children that naturalists keep track of how plants and animals change as they grow. Invite children to share ways their families and doctors keep track of how much they grow. If children mention being measured, help them think about ways they might measure their plants' growth by asking questions such as the following:

- *How could we measure this plant?*

- *Can you show me how you might measure this plant with string?*

- *What about this plant with the curved stem? How do we measure that?*

After a child or two has suggested or demonstrated ways you might keep track of the plants' changing height, focus the discussion on ways to keep track of changes in plants' development by asking a question such as the following:

EXAMPLE:

> ## WHAT OUR PLANTS LOOK LIKE
> ─────────────
> * They have leaves.
>
> * They are green.
>
> * Some have buds now.

> ## HOW OUR PLANTS WILL CHANGE
> ─────────────
> * They'll get big.
>
> * They'll have more leaves.
>
> * It might grow into a beanstalk.

Charts like these can help children reflect on changes over time. Add photos or children's drawings to illustrate their words.

Observational drawing is an essential feature of "Discovering Nature." One way to focus children's observations and thinking on growth and development is to help them compile a journal of drawings and notes they make over time.

Young children can also collect data on their plants' growth and development by using nonstandard measures like those made with a piece of string or a strip of paper. In addition, they can use standard measures such as a ruler, unifix cubes, or another unit.

For more about young children and measurement, see *The Young Child and Mathematics,* by Juanita Copley (NAEYC, 2000).

- *What happens if one of our plants grows a new leaf or a flower bud begins to develop?*

- *How will we keep track of those changes?*

If children do not suggest using photographs or observational drawings, make these suggestions yourself. Then ask, "What kinds of changes do you think we'll see in the photographs or drawings?"

EXPLORE

Observe plants and track their growth and development during choice times, at least once a week, or for as long as children's interest lasts. If possible, give the children the opportunity to see plants develop flowers, fruits, and seeds.

Encourage children to notice changes in their plants' growth and development.

Sit with a small group of children at the plant center. Encourage them to notice the ways the different seeds, bulbs, and cuttings planted in step 1 have grown and changed.

- *Do you think our cuttings have changed? What makes you say that?*

- *What's happening to the seeds we planted? What do you think will happen to them next?*

Help each child find and look at a seedling, bulb, or cutting they planted during step 1. Encourage them to measure the plant and think about ways they will track the plant's growth over time.

Focus children on changes in plants' height, width, or leaf size:

- *This piece of string shows us how tall the plant is today.*

- *What do you think we'll find when we measure the plant with string next week?"*

Guide children to look for changes in plants' development:

- *The last time we looked at this plant it had three leaves on it—now how many does it have?*

- *We took this photo of the plant last week—the leaves were bright green. Do the leaves look the same to you now?*

Record the changes.

Encourage children to use measuring string, observational drawing, and photographs to record changes in plants' growth and development.

Growth

- Children can keep track of their plant's height, width, and leaf size. Common early measuring tools include string, paper strips, cloth measuring tapes, rulers, and sticks.

- Allow children to come up with their own ways of measuring plants. Encourage them to measure the plant's height, width, and leaf size.

> You can add to children's study of change over time with the following:
>
> - During the late winter and early spring, bring in twigs and branches from trees and bushes and put them in water so children can watch them sprout.
>
> - Bring a large patch of moss into the classroom. Place it on a tray and spray it with water daily. Invite children to use hand lenses to see how the moss changes from week to week.

- Use a chart to record plants' changing heights. Identify each plant that's being measured over time on the chart with a number or color that corresponds to its pot. Record the plant's height, width, or leaf size by drawing lines on the chart or gluing down strings cut to the measurement.

Development

Children can keep track of their plant's development. Depending on what kind of plant they are growing, they might focus on the way its color changes from one shade to another. Or they might notice the way new leaves appear and grow. They might notice developing flowers, fruits, or seed pods. Depending on the children's interests, encourage them to do one or more of the following:

- Draw or photograph the shape of the plant so they can compare any changes from week to week.

- Use colored pencils, crayons, or paint to represent the plant's color; as plants mature, their colors often darken.

- Draw or photograph a close-up section of the plant that seems to be developing especially quickly, such as a flower bud or new leaves.

Remind children to count the number of new leaves or flowers on their plant. They can record the number on their drawing or the photograph. If children are engaged in recording their observations, leave them to their work. If they want to talk about their work, ask them questions such as the following:

- *Do you think the leaves will be an even darker shade of green next week? What makes you say that?*

- *How many leaves do you think it will have next week? Why do you say that? Do you think it will ever have flowers? How do you know?*

Observe and Document

It is important to look for children's ideas about how or why plants grow and change as they do. Use the observation record forms to jot down the important parts of conversations you have with children about the following:

- Things they notice about plants' development

- Ideas they might share about why these changes occur

- Ways they might help plants grow

You will use these documents to assess children's learning (see "Observation and Assessment" on p. 119) and to guide reflective conversations, as described below.

Reflect

Lead small and large group science talks for ten to fifteen minutes once a week for as long as plants continue to grow and develop.

Issue: *Several of the children seem to be losing interest because they don't see changes every day.*

Response: You might try encouraging the children to observe once or twice a week instead of every day. That way they are more likely to have something to notice.

Example:

Noah: *(Looks at plant.) It's dying.*

Teacher: *You think the plant is dying. Why do you say that?*

Noah: *The leaves.*

Teacher: *What about the leaves—have they changed?*

Noah: *They're not green.*

Teacher: *How have the leaves changed?*

Noah: *Now they're yellow.*

This child has clearly noticed the yellow leaves. He equates green leaves with life and yellow leaves with death.

Example: Sharing a drawing like this may encourage others to draw. For example, after Arthur shared his pumpkin drawing, several other children were eager to draw pictures of their plants too.

Conduct small group science talks.

Sit with a small group of children who have been interested in their plant's growth and development. Invite them to share the records they've been keeping. You might say the following:

- *Tell us the story of your growing plant. What did it look like when it was planted? How has it changed?*

- *How do you know it's grown?*

- *What do you think it will look like when it grows some more?*

Invite the other children to compare their observations with those who have shared. Ask questions such as the following:

- *Ben said his plant's leaves got longer but not fatter. What did you notice when you measured your plant's leaves, Ella? What do you think will happen to its leaves as the plant grows bigger?*

- *Do any of you have plants that are growing flowers? What are you noticing? When did you first notice them? What did they look like? What do you think will happen to them next?*

Encourage children to share their drawings and photographs, or refer to the measurement graph as they make their comparisons.

Look at books about plants.

Use reference books to help children reflect on their observations about plants. At any time in the schedule, encourage children to compare what they see in the books to what they have observed with their plants.

- *How is this tulip plant like your narcissus plant? What's different about them?*

- *What do you think the tulip needs to grow and stay healthy? How is that like your narcissus plant?*

Conduct a large group science talk.

Facilitate a science talk to help children share their developing theories about how plants grow and develop. Use your notes and children's observational drawings to help you focus on the questions children have about how plants change, and why. For example, share a child's drawing that illustrates what she thought the carrot top might look like once it had grown. Ask questions such as these:

- *How is the carrot top different from your drawing?*

- *What do you think made it grow?*

- *How do you think the carrot is going to change?*

Or, refer to your observational notes. If, for example, you noted that some children were fascinated to see roots growing out of their bean seeds before the leaves, ask the following:

- *Why do you think a plant's roots grow out of the seed before the leaves do?*

- *What do you think the root is for?*

ISSUE: *I prefer to work with children in small groups. So why would I do science talks with the whole group?*

RESPONSE: Small group discussions give each child a chance to contribute ideas and discuss with others, which is harder to do with a large group. But whole-group science talks are a time for children to hear *many* different ideas that may broaden their thinking and their understandings.

REMINDER

As children monitor plants' growth and development, be sure to bring children outdoors to make tree or bush observations once a month. See step 4 of "Focused Exploration: Plants" (p. 72).

Step 3: Plants and Their Parts

As children observe indoor and outdoor plants over time, they will begin to notice, discuss, and compare specific parts of plants. The goal of this step is to help children understand plants as made up of distinct parts that work together to form living structures that grow and develop. Learning the names of parts and exactly what they do is not the objective, although learning the vocabulary will help children talk with one another. To emphasize how the parts are related to the whole, start with what children have learned to this point. Suggest that children look at stems, trunks and branches, leaves, and roots, in that order.

First, as children focus on stems and branches, they can observe the structure or skeleton of the tree, the many ways plants are supported, and the ways they grow above ground. Then, when they focus on leaves, the plant parts attached to the branches, they can observe the variety of interesting shapes, sizes, colors, and textures leaves come in. Finally, children study roots, the structures that anchor and hold plants upright and that supply water and nutrients to the rest of the plant.

You and the children may see flowers, seeds, and fruits appear on plants indoors and outdoors. Children will likely be captivated by these beautiful and changing plant parts and will want to look closely at them too. The guide provides ways you can help children focus on plants' growth and development. If possible, try to grow some plants from seed to flower so children can experience the entire life cycle. This can be hard to do in the classroom, but it's worth a try.

Stems, Trunks, and Branches

Stems, trunks, and branches are the parts of a plant that support the entire structure. As children gain experience observing plants, they will begin to see differences between the usually softer stems of the indoor plants and the generally woody stems of outdoor trees (tree trunks are stems) and bushes. Also, children will begin to form ideas about the purposes of stems and how they grow and change over time.

Core Experiences

- ☐ Look at stems, trunks, and branches of plants indoors and outdoors.
- ☐ Compare different stems, trunks, and branches.
- ☐ Develop ideas about what stems, trunks, and branches are for; and record data about each.

Preparation

Identify an area with a variety of plants to observe—ideally, trees, bushes, weeds, grasses, or flowers. (See pp. 121–122 for safety guidelines.)

SCHEDULE

Set schedule for the next two weeks:

☐ 5–10 minutes for a meeting before each choice time and each outdoor observation

☐ 45–60 minutes for choice time, until all interested children have observed and represented plant stems

☐ 20–30 minutes for outdoor observation of plant stems, trunks, and branches, two or more times

☐ 10–15 minutes for a reflective science talk, once a week

MATERIALS

☐ Materials to start new plants (See "Growing and Caring for Plants," p. 127)

☐ 6 naturalist kits

☐ Ball of string and a pair of scissors

☐ Paints, markers, and pencils that represent the colors of the plants children are observing

☐ Clipboards with paper

☐ Collage materials that approximate the kinds of stems, trunks, and branches: pipe cleaners, wire, cardboard strips, and sandpaper

☐ Styrofoam pieces for the bases of wire sculptures, about 4 by 4 inches

☐ Plywood pieces for the bases of clay or plasticine sculptures, about 4 by 4 inches (See suggestions for long-term representation projects on p. 137.)

☐ Copies of the observation record form (p. 143) and the document annotation form (p. 144)

☐ Chart labeled "Stems, Trunks, and Branches"

FAMILY CONNECTIONS

Suggest families make rubbings of two or three tree trunks in their neighborhood. They might want to cut the rubbings into three-inch squares, shuffle the pieces, and play a matching game. Provide questions for adults to ask as they make the rubbings and play the game. For example, parents might ask questions like these:

- *Do you remember which tree this rubbing came from? How do you know?*
- *How did the bark feel?*
- *How are these rubbings similar? How are they different?*

TEACHING PLAN

ENGAGE

Introduce the study of stems, trunks, and branches for ten to fifteen minutes.

> **ISSUE:** *How do I explain what these plant parts do?*
>
> **RESPONSE:** It is usually not helpful to simply tell children about the role of stems or other parts. What is important is to provide children with many opportunities to explore so they can develop and refine their ideas. Ask questions like, "What do you think the stem is for?" or "Why do you think plants have stems?" to encourage children to share their ideas about what plant parts can do, and hear the ideas of others.

Introduce study.

Gather your children together in a circle and introduce the study of plant parts. Show them houseplants and some of the plants you started from seeds, bulbs, or cuttings earlier in the exploration. Ask the group if they know the names of any plant parts and what those parts do. Ask questions such as the following:

- *Look at these plants. What different parts do you see?*

- *Let's look at the parts of the plant that support it. Which part do you think holds the plant up?*

- *Let's look closely at these plants' stems. What do the stems do for the plant?*

- *Which part of your body does that?*

- *How are the stems alike? How are they different?*

- *Do trees have stems? Does anyone know what we call them?*

- *What are branches for?*

Use words and drawings to record children's ideas on the "Stems, Trunks, and Branches" chart.

Prepare children for indoor and outdoor explorations.

- Tell children that as naturalists, they are going to look carefully at stems, trunks, and branches.

- If you are preparing children for an indoor exploration, tell them that naturalist tools, including measuring string and scissors, will be available at the plant center to examine the stems and other parts of their plants.

- If you are preparing children for an outdoor exploration, tell them that you will bring their naturalist kits outdoors, and that you will bring a ball of string and a pair of scissors. Ask them what they think the string and scissors might be for. After they've offered their ideas, tell them that the string is for measuring the lengths of different stems outdoors. They might want to measure around a trunk or branch, or they might want to measure the height of a wildflower's stem.

EXPLORE

Observe stems, trunks, and branches outdoors and in the plant center, two or more times per week, for as long as children remain interested.

Encourage children to look closely.

At the plant center, or outdoors, encourage children to look closely at stems, trunks, and branches. Consider the following:

- Model being a naturalist. Look closely at stems, trunks, and branches, perhaps with a hand lens.

- Invite children to use their measuring string to compare the length of different stems or the circumference of different trees.

- Sit with children as they examine plants, and encourage them to observe, describe, and draw their observations by asking questions such as the following:
  - *What does the stem feel like? Is it soft? Is it straight? How does it move in the wind?*
  - *What about the tree trunk. How does it feel? Do you see or hear it moving?*
  - *Which plants have branches?*
  - *How do you think it helps the plant?*

Encourage children to represent what they notice.

Guide children's representation by using strategies like these:

- Sit with children and invite them to draw or paint one of the classroom plants. Remind them that they can choose colors that resemble the plants.

- As you sit with children, encourage them to look carefully at a nearby plant. Invite them to choose collage materials that look like the stem, branches, or trunk of the plant. Support them as they choose materials by asking questions such as these:
  - *You were telling me how bumpy the tree trunk felt. Which paper will you use to help us remember how it feels?*
  - *The tree's branches aren't the same color as its trunk. What will you use to make the branches?*

Talk with children about their representations.

- *Tell me about the stem on this plant.*

- *Why did you choose the pipe cleaner to represent it?*

Use the document annotation form to highlight what children's representations and conversations reveal about their inquiry skills and their understanding of science concepts.

Observe and document children's experiences, observations, and ideas.

As children explore stems, trunks, and branches, encourage them to collect information about these plant parts.

- When you see children feeling, counting, measuring, or using their fingers to trace stems, trunks, or branches, capture these moments with photos. Use the observation forms to record what children say and do.

- Listen for and record children's ideas about what stems, trunks, and branches are for.

Use this information to focus upcoming science talks.

REFLECT

Share observations and ideas about stems, trunks, and branches in group meetings for ten or fifteen minutes.

EXAMPLE: Tricia made a tree collage using paper, wire, and cardboard. Then she talked about the collage with her teacher.

Teacher: *Which part of your collage is the branch?*

(Tricia points to wire.)

Teacher: *Why did you choose wire to make the branch?*

Tricia: *'Cause it bends.*

This conversation reveals that Tricia carefully chose materials that represented the shape and flexibility of the tree she was making.

EXAMPLE:

STEMS, TRUNKS, BRANCHES

* Branches look like reindeer horns (Kathy)

* They're sticks (Marcus)

* Outdoors, they are brown (Elana)

* Indoors they are green and yellow (Joshua)

A chart like this records children's early impressions. As the exploration continues, refer back to the chart so children can revisit some of their earlier thoughts. Add to the chart, noting new observations and ideas. Even if children can't read it, they will be able to recognize their words when you read it.

Conduct small group discussions after outdoor explorations.

After children have had a chance to observe stems, trunks, and branches, help them to recall some of their observations. Ask questions such as the following:

- *How can you make your body look like the stem of a dandelion? The bottom branch of a willow tree? The trunk of an oak tree?*

- *What shape are the stems? What color? What do they feel like? How are they different? How are they the same?*

- *Why do you think plants have stems? What makes you think that?*

Conduct a science talk with a large group.

After all interested children have had a chance to explore stems, trunks, and branches, bring them together in a circle. Encourage them to compare the plants' parts to their own bodies by asking questions such as the following:

- *Do we have parts of our bodies that are like stems? Trunks? Branches? Why do you say so?*

- *Do stems move? How do you know?*

Invite children to use their bodies to make the shapes of various plants they know. For example:

- The tree or bush the group is studying

- Certain plants in the classroom

- A plant they can see from the classroom window

Tell the children that a pretend wind is going to blow through the classroom. Invite them to use their bodies to move like the tree or bush you're studying. Help them think about how the different stems, trunks, and branches respond to wind by asking questions such as these:

- *Which of our plants might bend the most in the wind? Why do you say that?*

- *Which might not move much at all? Why do you say that?*

Help children reflect on their observations and understandings.

Begin by reading the "Stems, Trunks, and Branches" chart to remind children of their observations and ideas. Refer to photos and children's representations as you encourage children to share additional observations they've made and ideas they're forming about how stems, trunks, and branches help plants. Ask questions such as the following:

- *Why do you think plants have stems, branches, and trunks? What do you think they do for the plant? How can you tell?*

- *What do you think would happen if they didn't have stems, trunks, or branches?*

Highlight new ideas by using a different color marker to record children's responses on the "Stems, Trunks, and Branches" chart.

Communicating observations and ideas is an inquiry skill. Movement is one mode of communication that allows nonverbal children to participate. Through movement, children can express what they have noticed and what they understand about plants.

EXAMPLE: I asked Maria what the long, skinny parts were on her apple tree. She said they were branches. This drawing really shows how Maria focused on the branches of the tree and how they held the apples.

"This is apple tree"

REMINDER

As children study plants' stems, trunks, and branches, be sure to bring children outdoors to make tree or bush observations once a month. See step 4 of "Focused Exploration: Plants" (p. 72).

Examining Leaves

Leaves, like flowers, are often the most distinguishing part of a plant. By looking more carefully at leaves—their different sizes, shapes, textures, and colors—children will be engaged in initial experiences with variation and diversity of living things. As they watch plants over time, they may see growth and development. Depending on the part of the country, they may also be able to explore dramatic changes in spring and fall.

CORE EXPERIENCES

□ Look at and collect leaves outdoors.

□ Compare leaves from the same kinds of plants found both indoors and outdoors.

□ Compare leaves from different kinds of plants.

□ Record data about leaves.

PREPARATION

Create a space for children's drawings and a place to keep leaf collections.

SCHEDULE

□ 5–10 minutes before each choice time or outdoor exploration

□ 45–60 minutes for choice time to observe, compare, and represent leaves, until all interested children have had opportunities

□ 20–30 minutes for outdoor exploration, once or twice a week

□ 10–15 minutes for a science talk, once a week

MATERIALS

□ 6 naturalist kits

□ 6 bags for collecting leaves

□ String for measuring leaves

□ Camera, if possible

□ Chart labeled "Leaves"

□ Copies of the observation record form (p. 143) and the document annotation form (p. 144)

FAMILY CONNECTIONS

Send suggestions, such as the following, home to families so they might talk with their children about leaves.

□ Go on a leaf scavenger hunt to see how many different kinds you can find.

□ Collect fallen leaves, two of each kind; mix them up and play a matching game.

□ Collect fallen leaves and put them in piles according to different attributes: color, size, or shape.

TEACHING PLAN

ENGAGE

Introduce the leaf study in a meeting with the whole group for five to ten minutes.

Introduce the study of leaves.

Sit with your whole group in a circle and display different kinds of classroom plants. Use your "Stems, Trunks, and Branches" chart to remind children of what they know about those plant parts. Then focus observations of leaves by asking questions such as the following:

- *What have you noticed about leaves?*
- *How are the leaves the same? How are they different?*
- *Why do you think plants have leaves?*
- *Have you ever seen a plant without leaves? Why didn't it have leaves?*

Use words and pictures to record children's ideas on the "Leaves" chart.

Prepare children for indoor and outdoor explorations.

Tell children that, as naturalists, they will observe, represent, and measure leaves indoors during choice times, and outdoors during their naturalists' outings. Encourage children to think about how they can keep track of leaves' different sizes and shapes.

If you are preparing children for an outdoor exploration, tell them they can collect leaves they find on the ground, but should not pull leaves off of plants. Show them the naturalist kits you'll be bringing outdoors including clipboards and markers, field guides, measuring string, hand lenses, penlights, and the leaf collecting bags.

If you are preparing children for an indoor exploration, show them the field guides that feature leaves that will be at the plant center. Show them the drawing and collage materials they can use to represent different leaves' colors, shapes, and textures.

After children have had a chance to observe leaves, help them to recall some of their observations and predict what they might see. Read the "Leaves" chart and ask questions such as these:

- *What did you notice about leaves the last time you were at the plant center or on an outdoor exploration?*
- *Has anyone found a picture of one of the leaves in the field guide? Will you share it with us?*
- *Where have you seen the biggest leaves? The smallest?*
- *What kind of leaves do you think you'll find today?*

EXPLORE

Observe plants' leaves indoors and outdoors.

ISSUE: *My children just want to bring in lots and lots of leaves.*

RESPONSE: Teachers find that limiting the number and kinds of leaves children bring indoors helps to focus them on certain characteristics of leaves. For example: "You can bring in three leaves, and one of them has to be a color other than green."

EXAMPLE: I was amazed at how focused Sareena was on her drawing of leaves. Before she started, she used the magnifier to examine the first leaf. Then as she started to draw the second leaf, she stopped so she could really examine its shape and features.

Encourage children to observe and represent leaves.

Use a hand lens to observe leaves on trees, bushes, and plants, and leaves on the ground. Wonder aloud by saying things such as, "I found this leaf over here. I wonder where it came from. Do you think there are other trees around here that have leaves like these?"

Encourage children to use the hand lenses and penlights. Invite children to describe and compare the leaves they find by saying things such as, "Look at the leaf Taikisha found! Does anyone else have a leaf that looks like that?"

- Draw a leaf and encourage children to do the same.
- Invite children to use a field guide and compare the pictures to the leaves they have found.

Encourage children to observe and represent the same plants from week to week. This will be of particular interest during times that leaves undergo changes, such as with new plants when they turn brown in the fall or shrivel due to lack of water.

Also, make a special trip to look at the leaves of the tree or bush that your children will be studying.

Encourage children to observe and compare leaves indoors.

Choose three or four plants from your indoor collection, each with different color, size, or textured leaves. As you sit with children observing these plants, help children describe and compare their leaves by asking questions such as these:

- *What are some ways these leaves look the same? Different?*
- *How can you describe the colors you see on the leaves?*
- *How can you describe their shapes?*
- *How do they feel when you touch them?*
- *What do you think the edges look like?*
- *Are all the leaves the same size?*

Place three or four bean plants, each at a different stage of development, at the plant center. Encourage children to notice the differences in their leaves by asking questions such as the following:

- *Are all the leaves the same?*
- *How are they different?*
- *What do you think they'll look like when they grow some more?*

Put a tray of leaves, collected outdoors, at the plant center. Make sure there are leaves from different types of plants. Have children group them in any way they want. Then ask questions such as the following:

- *What's the same about the leaves in this pile you made?*
- *Can you think of another way to group them?*

Encourage children to notice the variety of types as well as the variation among types by asking questions:

A book such as *Plant* from the Eyewitness Books series (Alfred A. Knopf) has wonderful photographs. Use books such as these to encourage children to look more closely at their own leaves.

These questions help children experience math concepts such as shape, size, and symmetry, as well as the science concepts of variation, diversity, and structure/function relationships.

EXAMPLE: Beth made a drawing of a leaf today. She talked about circles and I wrote down what she said. Tomorrow I plan to follow up with her, asking her what the circles were about.

These are the holes and this is the lines. I put the lines because the color don't go inside the hole part. The green keeps the color.

- *Can you find leaves that are the same?*
- *Are any exactly the same? How? or Why not?*
- *How many different kinds of leaves can you find?*
- *How are they different from one another?*

Have books about leaves and plants available at the book corner or at the plant center. Encourage children to compare the pictures in the books to the leaves they are observing. Add children's observations to the "Leaves" chart.

Encourage children to record and represent their observations about leaves.

- Invite children to trace or draw pictures of some of the leaves they have collected.
- Provide string and graph paper to compare and record leaves' sizes.
- Invite children to make a collage of a plant they have been observing. Encourage them to choose collage papers that represent the leaves' colors and texture. Show them how to tear or cut the papers to represent the leaves' shapes.
- Encourage children to become their plant and pretend they're enjoying a calm sunny day, and then a windy day.

Observe and document children's experiences, observations, and ideas.

As children observe plants indoors and out, use the observation forms to record how children explore and what they notice about leaves—their shapes, sizes, colors, textures, and placement on the plant.

Use the information to decide how to guide the study of leaves. For example, if children are noticing galls on leaves, give them opportunities to collect, sort, and research these leaves, while they think about the reasons leaves have galls. If they are interested in finding the smallest or largest leaves around, provide them with opportunities to collect big leaves, measure and research them, and think about why trees might have such big leaves.

REFLECT

Share observations and ideas about leaves in a science talk with a large group for ten to fifteen minutes.

Conduct a science talk in a large group each week to discuss children's observations and ideas about leaves.

Gather the whole group together to reflect on their observations and understanding of leaves as parts of plants. Begin by reading the leaves chart to the children to remind them of some of their initial observations and ideas.

Next, use photographs and children's representations to help children reflect on their observations. To focus the discussion, ask questions such as the following:

- *What have you noticed about leaves? Their shapes?*

Galls are growths on the outsides of leaves and stems of plants. They are caused by a number of different insects.

EXAMPLE: When Ethan shared his drawing, Cesarina asked him if it was a drawing of leaves or a drawing of trees. Ethan said, "Both." Then we looked more closely and noticed that Ethan had drawn both! His leaf has veins and is shaped like an oak leaf. His trees are round and have a few hidden branches. Our conversation proceeded to focus on the differences between leaves and trees!

ISSUE: *Only a few of my children participate in large group talks.*

RESPONSE: One way teachers have found to include more children in science talks is to address children by name and ask for their opinion or experience. For example: "Paul, what did you notice when we were looking closely at our tree's leaves?" Even if children do not participate in these discussions, they will benefit by hearing the ideas of others.

REMINDER

Be sure to bring children outdoors once a month to make tree or bush observations. See step 4 of "Focused Exploration: Plants" (p. 72).

- *How do leaves change? Why do you think they change?*
- *What changes have you noticed in leaves on our tree? On our classroom plants?*
- *Why do you think trees have leaves? What makes you say that?*
- *What would happen if they didn't have leaves? What's the difference between a dead tree and one that's lost its leaves for the winter?*

Use a different color marker to record children's new ideas on the "Leaves" chart.

Roots

The roots are an important part of the plant's structure. Without them, the wonderful parts children see could not stand up and survive. Roots, of course, are underground and not typically visible. However, when children are given opportunities to germinate seeds in paper towels, transplant seedlings, weed a garden, or dig up plants for a terrarium, they will have opportunities to observe roots and develop their own ideas about the purpose of roots.

CORE EXPERIENCES

☐ Look at roots of plants begun indoors.

☐ Compare roots of different kinds of plants.

☐ Look outdoors for roots.

☐ Develop ideas about the purpose of roots.

☐ Record data about roots.

PREPARATION

Germinate bean seeds on paper towels and grow seedlings in plastic bottles. (See p. 128.)

SCHEDULE

Set schedule for the next two weeks:

☐ 5–10 minutes for a meeting with the whole group before each choice time or outdoor exploration

☐ 45–60 minutes for choice time, two or three times a week

☐ 20–30 minutes for outdoor exploration, two or three times a week

☐ 10–15 minutes for a science talk, once a week

MATERIALS

☐ 6 naturalist kits

☐ Ball of string and scissors

☐ Camera, if possible

☐ Chart labeled "Roots"

☐ Copies of the observation record form (p. 143) and the document annotation form (p. 144)

Family Connection

Send home instructions for sprouting seeds and forcing cuttings and bulbs in water so families can observe root growth at home too.

Teaching Plan

Engage

Introduce the focus on roots in a discussion with the whole group for five to ten minutes.

Introduce the focus on roots.

Sit with your whole group in a circle and introduce them to the focus on roots. Begin by showing them some of the bean seeds you have germinated, bulbs you have forced, or cuttings you have put in water. Ask children what they notice about the plants' roots. Record their responses using pictures and words on the "Roots" chart.

Also, invite children to tell you about the times they've seen roots while gardening, digging for worms, moving bushes, and so on. Help children share some of their initial ideas about why plants have roots by asking questions such as the following:

- *Why do you think plants have roots?*

- *What do you think the roots are for?*

- *What do you think would happen if plants didn't have roots?*

- *What makes you say that?*

Add the children's ideas to the "Roots" chart.

> *Root viewers* help children look more closely at roots. For information about purchasing root viewers, check out the section on purchasing materials on p. 129.

Prepare children for indoor and outdoor explorations of roots.

If you are preparing children for their first outdoor exploration of plants' roots, suggest they plan to dig or pull up two or three weeds to observe and compare the roots. Show them the naturalist kits you'll be bringing outdoors. Remind them they can use the following:

- Clipboards and markers to draw their weeds with their roots

- Field guides to compare their weed's roots to the guide's drawings

- Hand lenses and penlights to help them look very closely at the roots

- Trowels to dig up weeds that are too hard to pull up

If you are preparing children for their first indoor exploration of plants' roots, show children select plants from the plant center:

- Bean seeds germinating on paper towels

- Seedlings growing in clear plastic bottles

- Cuttings, avocado pits, and narcissus bulbs rooting in clear containers of water

Also, remind children of the naturalist tools available for observing and recording: hand lenses, penlights, observational drawing materials, and measuring string.

EXPLORE

Observe plants' roots, outdoors and indoors.

Encourage children to look closely at plants' roots outdoors.

Take children outdoors to look at the class tree or bush. Help them think about its roots by asking questions such as the following:

- *Where do you think its roots are?*
- *What do you think they look like?*
- *How deep do you think they go?*
- *What shape do you think they are? Why do you say that?*

Encourage children to make observational drawings of the tree or bush, or other plants they're interested in, and encourage them to include the roots too. Show interested children illustrations of complete plants in field guides so they can see what their plants' roots look like. If weeds are available, continue to invite children to dig them up and draw the whole plant. They may want to bring the plants indoors to add to a terrarium.

Encourage children to look closely at plants' roots indoors.

Help children focus their observations on the growing roots of germinated seeds and the seedlings you started in plastic bottles (see "Preparation" above) as well as any cuttings you might have in your classroom collection. Ask questions such as the following:

- *How would you describe these roots?*
- *What do you think they'll look like when they grow more?*
- *What do you think roots are for?*

Record children's responses, using words and pictures, on the "Roots" chart.

Encourage children to record and represent their observations about roots.

You might invite children to look back at the plants they've been representing in collage. Ask them to imagine what their plants' roots might look like. Offer them string, raffia, or other materials that resemble roots, which they can glue or tape to their collages to represent their ideas. Help interested children graph the growth of a bean plant's roots.

Observe and document children's experiences, observations, and ideas about roots.

As children observe plants indoors and out, take photos and use the observation form to record how children explore and what they think

When you are out walking with your children, keep your eyes open for visible roots. Whether in a forest or in an urban area, you might find a tree that has fallen or been dug up, exposing roots. Seeing the roots attached to the trunk will help children connect the two.

EXAMPLE: Raffia was the perfect material for this child's collage because its flexibility and its different widths reminded her of the roots she had seen.

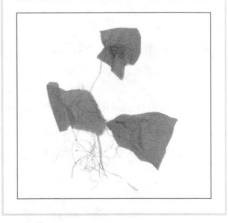

TEACHER NOTE: Three of the boys discovered the euonymus growing at the side of the school. They were fascinated by its roots—the way they grow right out of the stems. Now they're checking all of our various ground cover for rootlets!

or notice about roots. You will use the information to decide how to guide the focus on roots. For example, if children are noticing that some weeds' roots are long and thin and others aren't, give them opportunities to collect, sort, and research different kinds of roots. If they are interested in finding out which roots grow faster—a bean plant's or an avocado's—provide them with opportunities to measure and record the roots' growth over time.

Create a documentation panel of the classroom plants' root growth and development.

Use your photographs and children's work to create a documentation panel that shows how the roots of a plant grew over time. Include a sentence about how children are using their observation skills to deepen their understanding of plant parts. See the guidelines for creating documentation panels on p. 142. You will use this panel for upcoming science talks.

REFLECT

Share observations and ideas about roots and their function during a science talk with a large group for ten to fifteen minutes.

Conduct a science talk with a large group.

Once a week, gather the whole group together to share and reflect on their observations of roots. Begin by reading the "Roots" chart to help children remember their earlier experiences. Refer to photos and children's representations as you encourage children to share additional observations and ideas about roots. To focus the discussion, ask questions such as the following:

- *What are some things we've noticed or learned about roots?*
- *Do you think all plants have roots? What makes you say that?*
- *Do you think all roots look the same? Why or why not?*

Encourage children to compare roots to parts of their bodies.

Ask questions such as the following:

- *Do we have parts of our bodies that are like roots?*
- *How would you make your body look like one of the plants you've been studying, including its roots? Can you show me what parts would move when it rains or gets windy?*

Help children share their ideas and theories about why plants have roots.

Invite children to share their ideas about why plants have roots. Their theories may be based on misunderstandings, but that is developmentally appropriate. Misunderstandings should not be "corrected." Instead, help children examine their theories with follow-up questions. For example, if a child suggests plants have roots to give them food, ask them what kind of food they think plants get with their roots or how the roots get the food to the rest of the plant.

EXAMPLE: I asked Alexis to share her drawing as a way of beginning our science talk. Now everyone wants to share their drawings! I think I'll set up a couple of root drawing tables if their interest continues.

EXAMPLE: Jamal made an observational drawing of an oak tree seedling. He was convinced the acorn seed was a worm. When I asked if the worm moves, he held the seedling up and turned it all around: "Hmm, the worm is gone! There's an acorn there, instead."

REMINDER

As children study plants' roots, be sure to bring children outdoors to make tree or bush observations once a month. See step 4 (p. 72).

Use a different color marker to record children's responses on the "Roots" chart, highlighting their new observations and ideas.

Flowers

Your indoor and outdoor plants may or may not offer children opportunities to observe and compare flowers. If your children can observe plants that have fascinating, beautiful, and often fast-changing parts, you can help them begin to understand one of their important roles—to attract insects. Insects pollinate plants, and seeds begin to develop.

CORE EXPERIENCES

- ☐ Look at flowers.
- ☐ Compare flowers.
- ☐ Develop ideas about the purpose of flowers.
- ☐ Record data about flowers.

PREPARATION

If your classroom plant collection includes budding or flowering plants, pick out a few for children to focus their observations on.

SCHEDULE

- ☐ 5–10 minutes for a meeting before each choice time or outdoor exploration
- ☐ 20–30 minutes for outdoor exploration, once or twice during the week, depending on the availability of flowering plants for children to observe
- ☐ 45–60 minutes for choice time to observe, compare, and represent leaves, until all interested children have had opportunities
- ☐ 10–15 minutes for a science talk

MATERIALS

- ☐ 6 naturalist kits, including field guides of local flowering plants
- ☐ Collage materials such as tissue paper and pipe cleaners
- ☐ Drawing materials (crayons, markers, or colored pencils)
- ☐ Several cut flowers
- ☐ 6 clipboards

FAMILY CONNECTION

- ☐ Make a special request for flower gardeners to visit the classroom and share their experiences, tools, and, if possible, some flowers.
- ☐ Let families know about your focus on flowers and suggest they

For the purposes of this exploration, provide children with opportunities to observe both cut flowers and flowers attached to plants. That way you can help to keep the focus on plant as a whole made up of many parts including flowers. Clearly, this exploration is best done when children can see flowers blooming outdoors. In most parts of the country, spring and summer are ideal.

take walks with their children to look at the different kinds of flowering plants they see in the neighborhood.

Teaching Plan

Engage

Introduce the focus on flowers in a meeting for five to ten minutes with the whole group.

Introduce the focus on flowers.

Bring children together in a circle to talk about the flowers. Tap their interests and experiences by sharing a couple of cut flowers or flowering plants. Ask some of the following questions:

- *Have you seen these parts of plants before? Where?*
- *What have you noticed about what they look like? How they smell? Where do they grow?*

If children do not use the word, you can introduce the word *flower*. Help them explore their ideas about flowers by asking questions such as the following:

- *How do you think the flower got there?*
- *Do you think flowers change or grow?*
- *What do you think happens to the flower after it stops growing?*

Accept children's ideas, and record them on a chart.

Prepare children for indoor and outdoor exploration of flowers.

Tell children that as naturalists, they will observe and represent flowers indoors during choice times and, depending on your local environment, outdoors. Remind children they can use the naturalists' tools to look closely at plants and flowers and the field guides to learn more. Also remind children about materials they can use for representation:

- Show children the paints, colored pencils, crayons, or markers available for observational drawings of flowers and remind them that the drawing tools come in so many colors because flowers come in so many colors.
- Show children the collage materials available for making representations of flowers.

Explore

Observe flowers.

Encourage children to look closely at cut flowers in small groups.

- Give each child in a small group a cut flower or two to observe. If possible, give each child two different kinds of flowers so they can compare them.
- Offer children hand lenses and penlights to notice details.

> **Teacher note:** When the bean plants began to flower I posted pictures around the room from an old calendar of flowers. The kids noticed the new pictures when they came in this morning so it was the perfect time to begin our discussion of flowers

> Look for collage materials that lend themselves to representing flowers: tissue paper (petals) and pipe cleaners (stems).

- If possible, gently open up the flowers' stems or cut into their centers so children can see more.

- Wonder aloud and engage children in conversations about how the flowers are alike, how they are different, and what they might do for plants. You might say something such as the following:
  - *I wonder if this flower has as many petals as that one.*
  - *I wonder why these flowers are so colorful! How many colors do you see?*
  - *Do all of these flowers smell nice? I wonder why leaves don't smell like this!*

Refer to field guides and share them with children.

Keep some cut flowers in water and let children see them fade over time. Discuss with them their ideas about what they think is happening.

Encourage children to find and look closely at outdoor flowering plants.

- Look closely at flowers yourself. Notice their parts and colors.

- Use a hand lens and penlight to notice details and encourage children to do the same.

- Offer children clipboards and colored pencils or markers so they can make observational drawings of an outdoor flowering plant. Some children might want to draw the entire plant, bush, or tree, while others might choose to draw one flower.

- Wonder aloud and engage children in conversations about how the flowers are alike and different, what they might do for plants, and how they might change over time. You might say the following:
  - *I wonder if there are ants inside all of these peonies.*
  - *What colors do you see in these flowers?*

Encourage children to observe changes in flowering plants over time.

Use the following strategies:

- Indoors, place bean plants that are budding, flowering, and form-ing seed pods in the plant center, and invite children to look closely at the differences among the plants.

- If you've been taking photographs of a growing flowering plant, such as an amaryllis, glue the photos in chronological order on poster board and sit with children while they describe the way the flower develops.

- Outdoors, encourage children to draw the same flower every few days. Date the pictures so you and children can see how the flower changes over time.

Encourage children to represent what they notice about cut flowers and flowering plants.

Use the following strategies:

- Invite children to use paints, colored pencils, markers, or crayons to create observational drawings of cut flowers or flowering plants.

TEACHER NOTE: Mary brought daffodils to school. Now we're comparing them to our class geraniums.

Before you go outdoors to observe flowering plants, remind children that they are naturalists and should not pick flowers.

ISSUE: *My kids always seem to draw flowers the same way, sometimes even with smiley faces on them!*

RESPONSE: Drawing stylized and smiley-faced flowers is what young children do! You can be positive in your reaction to these stylized draw-ings as you talk with children about the differences between their draw-ings and the real flower in front of them. You might ask them how their drawing is different from the real flower. Your support and observa-tions about their drawings will help children capture important details.

- Invite children to make models of the cut flowers or flowering plants. Offer them collage materials that look like the flowers they've been observing. Talk with children about their models. Ask them why they chose to use the materials they did to construct their model.

- Later, use the document annotation forms to highlight what children's representations and words reveal about their inquiry skills and their understanding of science concepts.

Reflect

Share observations of flowers in science talks with large groups for ten to fifteen minutes.

Conduct science talks with a large group to discuss children's observations of flowers.

Each week during children's focus on flowers, gather the group together to reflect on their observations. Use children's observational drawings and any photographs you have of the flowers they have been observing to focus how they think about the various colors, shapes, and sizes of flowers.

Seeds

Children have seen plants grow from seed. Now you can help them begin to understand another important role plants have: producing seeds that grow into new plants. By giving children opportunities to dissect fruit, collect seeds, and compare different varieties, you will help them become aware of some of the many different seeds in their world.

Core Experiences

- ☐ Look at plants that are producing seeds.
- ☐ Look at the plant parts that hold the seeds.
- ☐ Develop ideas about a plant's life cycle.
- ☐ Record data about different seeds.

Preparation

Schedule

- ☐ 5–10 minutes for a meeting before each choice time or outdoor exploration

- ☐ 45–60 minutes for choice time to observe, compare, and represent seeds in their various forms, until all interested children have participated

- ☐ 20–30 minutes for outdoor exploration, once or twice during the week to observe plants and their seeds

Example: This drawing prompted an interesting discussion about where the pumpkin comes from. Gabriela seems to realize it's related to the flower. Others are not so sure.

Plants have many ways of reproducing. This exploration focuses on plants that reproduce by generating seeds and helps children begin to understand that seeds are produced in many different ways. Fruits contain seeds, vegetables do not—tomatoes, peppers, and cucumbers are technically fruits, not vegetables. Some fruits have hard shells, like peanuts and walnuts. Their seeds are called nuts. Pinecones are different from fruits even though they also produce seeds. Milkweed seeds come out of pods, maple trees produce hundreds of winged seeds, and a sunflower's seeds can be harvested right from the flower. Seeds are alike because they all contain an embryo and enough food for it to begin developing.

☐ 10–15 minutes for a science talk about plants and various kinds of seeds

MATERIALS

☐ Field guides of local trees and plants

☐ Collage materials such as cardboard (pinecone scales) or quilt batting (fluff on dandelion seeds)

☐ Crayons, markers, paints, or colored pencils

☐ Local fruit cut down the center, one for each child

☐ Tray for drying seeds

☐ Plant with a fruit or seed pod growing on it such as a bean, tomato, or zucchini plant, or an apple or orange tree

FAMILY CONNECTION

☐ Make a special request for vegetable gardeners to visit the classroom and share their experiences, tools, and, if possible, some edible fruits like peppers, tomatoes, and zucchini.

☐ Suggest that families and children keep a list of all of the different kinds of fruits they eat at home. They also might want to collect seeds from these fruits, dry them, and plant them at home.

TEACHING PLAN

ENGAGE

Introduce the focus on seeds for five to ten minutes in a meeting with the whole group.

Introduce the focus on seeds.

Bring children together outdoors around a fruit-bearing tree, a bush with berries, or a sunflower that has gone to seed. Or gather indoors in a circle around a fruit-bearing potted plant such as a pole bean or cherry tomato plant to talk about seeds. Tap their interest and experiences by asking the following questions:

- *Have you seen these parts of plants before? Where?*

- *What do you think they are for?*

If children do not use the words, you can introduce the words *fruit* and *seeds*. Help them explore their ideas about fruits and seeds by asking questions such as the following:

- *How do you think the tomato (acorn or berry) got there?*

- *Do you think all plants grow tomatoes (acorns or berries)? Why do you say that?*

- *What do you think happens to the tomato (acorn or berry) if no one eats it?*

> **TEACHER NOTE:** When the bean plants began to produce fruit, I brought in green beans from the grocery store and a package of bean seeds. I put them next to the bean plants and one child immediately made the connection.

Prepare children for indoor and outdoor exploration of seeds.

Tell children that as naturalists, they will observe and represent seeds indoors during choice times and outdoors. Remind children they can use the field guides to learn more.

EXPLORE

Observe seeds.

Encourage children to look closely at the seeds in cut fruits.

- Give each child in a small group a fruit with seeds in it that has been cut in half. If possible, give each child a different kind of fruit so seeds and fruits can be compared.

- Encourage children to remove the seeds from their fruit.

- Invite children to count the number of seeds they see in the different fruits. Offer them paper and markers to record their findings by drawing the fruit and recording the number in tally marks or with a numeral next to the drawing.

- Suggest children find the smallest seed and the largest seed at the table.

- Wonder aloud and engage children in conversations about the fruits and seeds. You might say the following:
  - *This grapefruit seed is already sprouting! What do you think will happen to it? Why do you say that?*
  - *I wonder if this apple has as many seeds as that one.*
  - *What do you think will happen if we plant this zucchini seed?*

Suggest children put their fruit seeds on a tray to dry out so they can be planted another day.

Also, invite children to eat the remaining fruit!

Plant fruit seeds.

After the seeds have dried out for three or more days, set up a small table with potting soil and a seed tray so children can plant seeds they have collected.

- Engage them in conversation about what they will need to do to help their plant grow.

- Ask them to describe or draw the kind of plant they think their seed will produce.

Encourage children to look for seeds outdoors.

Encourage children to look closely at trees, bushes, weeds, and on the ground for what they think might be seeds.

- When children find something they think is a seed but they aren't sure, ask them to tell you or show you why they think it might be a seed. Listen to their ideas.

- Use a field guide to look for information about the seeds that children find.

Before you go outdoors to observe plants with seeds, remind children that they are naturalists and should not pick fruits or seeds off of plants.

TEACHER NOTE: Children have been bringing in seeds from the fruits they eat at home. We're making a seed museum! The children are also getting excited about planting these seeds because they want to grow their own food!

- If fruits, nuts, or other seeds are on the ground, invite children to pick up one of each to bring indoors to look at more carefully.

- Wonder aloud and engage children in conversations about the fruits and seeds they find. You might say the following:
  - *I wonder if there are seeds inside this berry that fell off of the bush.*
  - *What do you think will happen to all of these acorns?*

Observe seeds collected from the outdoors.

During choice times, sit with children at small tables and talk with them about the collection of seeds they gathered outdoors. Suggest they sort the collection in a way that makes sense to them. Children might sort the seeds by color, size, kind, shape, or texture. Talk with them about how the seeds are alike and different.

Help children think about where the seeds came from and what might happen to them by asking questions such as the following:

- *How do you think this acorn got on the oak tree?*

- *What do you think happens to the milkweed seeds after they blow away?*

Encourage children to represent what they notice about fruits and seeds.

- Sit with children as they look for seeds in fruit and invite them to use paints, colored pencils, markers, or crayons to create observational drawings of what they see.

- Invite children to make models of the fruits, nuts, or seed pods they have collected. Talk with children about their models. Ask them why they chose to use the materials they did to construct their model.

Later, use the document annotation forms to highlight children's representations and words and what they reveal about their inquiry skills and their understanding of science concepts.

REFLECT

Share observations of flowers for ten to fifteen minutes in science talks with a large group.

Conduct a science talk with a large group to discuss children's focus on seeds.

After all interested children have had a chance to look closely at a variety of seeds, bring the whole group together to reflect on their observations.

Focus the discussion using children's observational drawings of plants with fruits or seeds attached, or any photographs you might have taken of these kinds of plants during your outdoor explorations. Help children share their observations and understandings by asking questions such as the following:

- *Where have you been finding seeds outdoors? Where do you think they come from?*

- *What do you think happens to the seeds in the berries and crab apples we've found?*

> Look for collage materials that lend themselves to representing fruits, nuts, and other seeds: pieces of corrugated cardboard resemble pinecone scales; small boxes can be painted like fruit; tissue paper inside the box resembles the fruit's flesh; and scraps from a hole punch become the fruit's seeds.

Step 4: Monthly Tree or Bush Observations

By observing a tree or bush regularly for a full year, children have the opportunity to focus very closely on a single plant, its characteristics, how it changes over time, which animals use it as part of their habitat, and much more. And, if the tree or bush flowers, grows fruit, goes to seed, or loses its leaves only to grow new ones, all the better! Children will have many changes to notice, record, and discuss, and they can connect these observations to their ongoing study of plants and animals. For example, as you study plant parts, always have the children look at the different parts of the tree or bush.

CORE EXPERIENCES

- ☐ Observe and keep a record of a tree or bush as it changes from month to month over a long period.
- ☐ Collect data on the tree or bush.
- ☐ Research the tree or bush.
- ☐ Discuss changes in the tree or bush.

Initial Tree or Bush Observation

PREPARATION

Identify at least one nearby tree or bush that might be interesting to observe over the course of the year. Think about whether it will have features that will change obviously, such as leaves that will change color or fall, or will have flowers or fruits. The tree or bush needs to be in a safe place where children can observe the tree, touch it, measure it, and draw it. Keep a record of the tree or bush's changes and what you and the children learn about it over time. Begin a class book and include monthly photographs and children's drawings of the tree or bush, written records of children's questions, their observations, and any information they find out about the tree by measuring it, counting its parts, reading about it, and questioning a guest arborist.

SCHEDULE

- ☐ 5–10 minutes for a meeting before the outdoor observation
- ☐ 15–20 minutes for outdoor observation
- ☐ 10–15 minutes for a science talk

MATERIALS

- ☐ Field guides
- ☐ 6 naturalist kits
- ☐ 6 clipboards and paper

☐ Crayons, markers, paints, or colored pencils

☐ Big blank book

☐ Camera, if possible

TEACHING PLAN

ENGAGE

Introduce the tree or bush study in a discussion with the whole group for five to ten minutes.

Introduce the tree or bush study.

Sit in a circle with the whole group to introduce them to the tree or bush study. Explain that as naturalists they will observe a tree or bush very closely all year long, to see how it changes and to find out as much as they can about it.

Tell the children where the tree or bush is located. Ask them if they ever remember noticing it, and if so, what they remember about it. Then invite them to go outside with you to look at it and see what they notice.

EXPLORE

Take children outdoors for their first tree or bush observation.

Look at the tree or bush outside.

Help children focus on being naturalists by using the following strategies:

- Have the group encircle the tree, and ask each child to describe something about it.
- Ask children if the tree or bush is like any they've ever noticed before, or if they think it will ever have flowers, lose its leaves, or blow over.
- Ask them what they would like to learn about the tree or bush. Record their questions and comments.

If you have a camera, take photos of the tree.

REFLECT

Share observations of the tree or bush in a science talk with the whole group for five to ten minutes.

Talk about the exploration.

Back in the classroom, bring your whole group together in a circle. Ask them what they liked about their tree or bush. Ask them to remind one another of some of the things they noticed about its size, shape, leaves, bark, or the animals living in or near it, and so on. Ask them how they think the tree or bush will change over the school year. Probe their thinking by asking why they think so. Read the list of things children wanted to find out about their tree or bush. Ask children if there is anything they want to add or change.

TEACHER NOTE: I decided to choose a bush to observe this year rather than a tree. The bush's branches are at the children's eye level, and it flowers in the spring! I took a photo of it, which I enlarged and brought to the meeting.

EXAMPLE: This is the first page of our tree book.

We began taking photographs of the maple tree in the park so we could observe how it changed over time.

Introduce the class tree or bush book.

Engage children in a conversation about naturalists as data collectors by asking a question such as, "How will we keep records of how our tree or bush changes from month to month?" Accept their ideas, and offer the following suggestions:

- Take photos and make drawings of the tree or bush once a month.

- Measure how big around the trunk is, or how high off the ground the first branch is.

- Collect parts that fall off of it: a few leaves, flowers, nuts, and so on.

Create a class book of observational drawings, notes, and photographs documenting the changes the children observe each month. Show children the big blank book and explain that it will be the book they'll use to keep track of how their tree or bush changes and what they learn about it, all year! Tell them that you're going to write the questions they have about their tree or bush in the book. Glue one of the photographs you took of the tree today on the first page too. Invite children to take turns decorating and signing their names on the book during your next choice time.

> **TEACHER NOTE:** I introduced the idea of a big tree book when we came in from our first visit. The children decided to put a drawing of the tree on the front with all of their names. Then on another page I wrote down kids' ideas about how the tree might change. Tomorrow I'll see if some kids want to make pictures of how they think the tree will look in the winter. Then I can record their ideas about why they think this will happen.

Ongoing Tree or Bush Observations

PREPARATION

This would be a good time to plan for an arborist to visit the classroom. See extensions on p. 110 for guidance.

SCHEDULE

- ☐ 5–10 minutes for a meeting before each monthly outdoor observation

- ☐ 15–20 minutes for monthly outdoor observations

- ☐ 10–15 minutes for science talks following each outdoor observation

MATERIALS

- ☐ Field guides

- ☐ Naturalist kits

- ☐ Collecting bags

- ☐ Class tree or bush book

- ☐ Clipboards with paper

- ☐ Markers

- ☐ Camera, if possible

- ☐ Copies of the observation record form (p. 143) and the document annotation form (p. 144)

TEACHING PLAN

ENGAGE

Make connections from one exploration to the next for five to ten minutes in a meeting with the whole group.

Connect last month's observation to current indoor and outdoor observations.

Bring the whole group together in a circle and help children reflect on their previous tree or bush observation(s) by reading and discussing the class tree or bush book. Jog children's memories by asking questions such as the following:

- *Is that what you remember, Nicole?*
- *What did you observe last month, Miguel?*

Help children predict changes they may notice by asking questions such as the following:

- *How do you think the tree or bush will look different this time?*
- *Why do you think it's made those changes?*

Help children make a connection between their current indoor and regular outdoor exploratory work with questions and comments such as the following:

- *You've been looking at lots of different plants outside. Which ones remind you of our tree or bush? How?*
- *You've been keeping track of the way the bean plant's leaves are growing. Do you think our tree or bush's leaves grew since the last time we looked at them? How will we know?*

Make plans for collecting more data.

Ask children what they'd like to learn or record about their tree during this visit. If you need to, offer them a list of choices, which could include the following:

- Draw the whole plant or parts of it.
- Measure the circumference of its trunk, the height of its lowest branch, or the length of its leaves.
- Take photos of the whole plant or parts of it.
- Collect fallen leaves, seeds, flowers, or fruits.
- Make bark rubbings.

Assign interested pairs of children to data collection tasks. Show the group the bag of naturalist tools you'll be taking outdoors with you.

- Field guide
- Clipboards and markers
- Measuring string
- Collecting bags

Explore

Observe and collect data about the tree or bush outdoors, once a month.

Encourage children to look closely.

Outdoors, encourage children to use their senses and naturalist tools to observe the tree or bush. Invite them to share their observations.

- *What changes do you see? Hear? Smell?*

- *Why do you think the tree or bush changed like that?*

- *I wonder if any animals live on or near the tree? Are the leaves changed in any way from the last time we were here? Look at the color of the bark!*

Sketch the tree and encourage children to do the same.

Connect children's observations to what they've noticed about indoor plants.

Connect what children are noticing outdoors to some things they've noticed about indoor plants: "Remember how the seeds we have indoors have roots? Can we find roots of this tree? Where might they be? Are leaves coming out of the tree the same way they have from the bean seed?"

Support children as they collect data.

Use strategies such as asking children which naturalist tool they would like to use and how they will use it. Or remind children of the possibilities:

- Make drawings of the whole plant

- Make drawings of the leaves, flowers, seed pods, and other parts

- Collect fallen leaves, seeds, or flowers

- Make bark rubbings

- Measure height of lowest branch

Read about the tree or bush from a field guide and compare its illustrations and information to what children are noticing.

Observe and document children's continuing exploration.

- Photograph or make sketches of the tree or bush to capture how it changes from month to month.

- Jot down snippets of children's conversations or words they use to describe what they see and wonder about.

- Use the observation forms to record what children say and do and how they collect and record data.

Use the document annotation forms to provide details about photos, conversations, or children's work samples. You will use this information, along with the records you've been collecting, for your upcoming science talks.

EXAMPLE: Sketching allows you to record what children observe. At the same time, you serve as a model for children, demonstrating what naturalists do as part of their work.

ISSUE: *Our bush doesn't change very much from month to month.*

RESPONSE: Some changes are very subtle and slow, and some plants lie dormant for months, which is all part of the growth pattern. So keep collecting data, even if it is the same for a couple of months. Eventually more obvious changes will occur!

REFLECT

Compare images of your tree over time for five to ten minutes during a science talk with the whole group.

Conduct a science talk in a large group.

After each monthly outdoor visit to your tree or bush, bring the whole group together and invite children to share their observations, drawings, measurements, and new questions. If possible, record the conversation on audiotape so you can review it and transcribe relevant bits to include in the class tree or bush book. Facilitate the conversation by saying something such as these:

- *We're going to add to our book about our tree or bush.*

- *I'm going to write down what you noticed about the tree or bush this time. What changes did you notice?*

Invite children to share their observational drawings: "Tell us about your drawing. What changes did you notice about our tree or bush?" Later, add these drawings to the class tree or bush book, and transcribe relevant pieces of the audio tape or interview children so you can add the words they use to describe their drawings.

Invite children who measured or counted to share their records:

- *How many apples did you see on the tree?*

- *How high was the lowest branch this time?*

- *How long were the leaves you measured?*

- *How many squirrels did you see in the tree?*

Invite children who collected leaves, seeds, cones, fruits, or flowers to share their collections: "Tell us about your collection. How are these items—leaves, flowers, fruits, seeds, and cones—alike? How are they different?"

Compare indoor and outdoor observations.

Help children compare what they have been learning about plant parts and needs to their tree or bush. Hold up an observational drawing or a three-dimensional representation of the indoor plants children are currently studying. Ask questions such as, "Lucy used a pipe cleaner to represent our avocado plant's stem. What will you choose from our collage materials to make our tree's trunk and branches? Why? How are the two stems different? How are they the same?"

Compare observations to previous monthly observations and discuss theories about any changes.

Help children share their ideas about why their tree or bush has changed, or not changed! Share a series of photographs that you have taken monthly of the tree or bush, or share a series of children's observational drawings.

This conversation will be based on children's naïve ideas, which is as it should be!

TEACHER NOTE: I'm using a bulletin board to display drawings and photos of our bush. It's divided into months so we can keep track of our monthly observations. The class book is great, but this gives us more room for the children's work.

TEACHER NOTE: I was amazed at mica's drawing and how carefully she drew the position of each leaf. Since we've been looking at the way leaves attach to stems, we compared mica's drawing to the way our bush's leaves attached to its branches.

- If, for example, a child suggests that their tree lost its leaves because it's fall, ask them, "How does it help the tree to lose its leaves in the fall?"

- If they suggest that there are spiders living in their bush because spiders think their bush is pretty, ask them, "What else is it about our bush that makes it a good home for spiders?"

- If children suggest their bush hasn't changed because it's dead, ask them, "How can you tell it's dead? How would you know if it were alive?"

focused exploration: animals

The focused exploration of animals builds on three- to five-year-olds' fascination with animals. Even if children aren't eager to touch or handle worms, snails, pill bugs, and mealworms initially, they love to watch them wiggle, dig, eat, or climb.

As children investigate animals in the outdoors, they will collect and record data, represent their observations and understandings, wonder about the ways animals' bodies and behaviors help to meet their needs, and share ideas and formulate theories about why particular animals look and behave the way they do.

To make close observations of animals possible, you and your children will also collect and house short-term visitors—such as bugs, worms, and snails—that you will then release. If you cannot find animals in your schoolyard, or if you want to provide children with opportunities to study an animal's life cycle, you can purchase animals to become long-term visitors. The section about essential information (pp. 121–130) provides guidance for finding, purchasing, and caring for your animal visitors.

Field trips to ponds, meadows, swamps, wet woods, or nature centers give children opportunities to observe and wonder about various kinds of animals. Guest experts who can share their knowledge about local animals and their habitats also give children new information about animals' lives. Books can enrich children's naturalist experiences by offering new information and stimulating new questions. The extension section (p. 107) suggests ways you can incorporate field trips, guest visitors, and books into this exploration. The guide also points out places where you can help children make connections between animals' and plants' lives: their needs and the ways their forms help them function and survive.

A naturalist environment must convey an attitude of serious respect for living things and their habitats. Outdoors this means disturbing the environment as little as possible; indoors this means moving from practices of keeping animals as pets to creating mini-environments in which living things are in as natural an environment as possible. While there are good reasons to kill some small animals, such as mosquitoes and ants, it is important to convey to children an interest in these animals and a respect for them. Be sure to talk with families, too, so they can be part of this effort.

See the section on science teaching (p. 115) for information about young children's inquiry and strategies you can use to focus and deepen their experiences and thinking during the exploration.

Step 1: Search for Animals

By recording where children find bugs, worms, and other small animals, you help them begin to notice that certain animals live in certain places. This provides the foundation for children's later understanding of habitats.

Core Experiences

- ☐ Look for animals outdoors.
- ☐ Help to record where animals are found.
- ☐ Think about animals' needs and how the environment helps to provide for those needs.

Preparation

- ☐ Do a safety check for broken glass, poison ivy, and other dangerous items in the outdoor area where children will be exploring. (See the safety guidelines on p. 121.)
- ☐ Display books about animals that children are likely to see outdoors.
- ☐ Display posters of animals that children are likely to see outdoors.

Schedule

Set schedule for the week:

- ☐ 5–10 minutes for a meeting before each outdoor exploration
- ☐ 30 minutes for outdoor explorations, once or twice a week
- ☐ 10–15 minutes for reflection after each outdoor exploration

Materials

- ☐ 6 naturalist kits
- ☐ Field guides
- ☐ 6 clipboards with paper

☐ Markers

☐ Camera, if possible

☐ Copies of the observation record forms (p. 143) and the document annotation forms (p. 144)

☐ Chart labeled "Animal Observations"

FAMILY CONNECTION

☐ Send home notes periodically about what children are doing and learning.

☐ Send home "Families Discovering Nature" (p. 132), which offers ideas for activities and thoughtful questions that caregivers can ask their children.

☐ Encourage family members to join you for the outdoor exploration.

TEACHING PLAN

ENGAGE

Introduce the animal study in a discussion with the whole group for five to ten minutes.

Share observations about animals.

Help children recall the animals they've been finding outdoors recently as well as where they found each animal by asking questions such as the following:

- *What animals have you seen outdoors recently?*
- *Where did you find the snail? Did you find snails on all the walls?*
- *Tanya found a spider on the tree's trunk. Brenda, where did you see a spider?*

Record what the children say, using pictures and words, on the animal observations chart.

If you have any pictures or children's artwork of animals, review those as well.

- *Jose, you drew this picture of a caterpillar last week. Do you remember where it was?*
- *Here's a photograph of Mirah when she found a worm. Do you remember where this is?*

If your terrarium has animals in it, help children think about where they might have come from: "When I made this terrarium for our classroom, I found a spider and a pill bug out in our yard to put in it. Which part of the yard do you think the spider was in? The pill bug?"

Make predictions.

- Explain that you will be taking children outdoors to do something naturalists do when they study animals: you will look for animals and use pictures and words to record what you find and where you find them.

EXAMPLE: When the teacher asked Adriel to share her drawing, Adriel said she drew the ants on the picnic table.

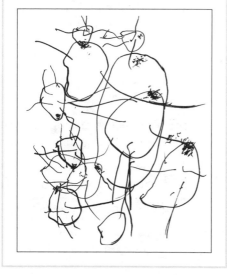

TEACHER NOTE: Almost half of the kids in my class are from different countries—from Africa to Haiti, from Russia to Japan. During the discussion, I realized that some of these kids have had experiences with animals other than those that live in our local environment. So I decided to get some field guides with animals from other parts of the world, so children who grew up in other countries can tell classmates about the animals they had observed.

- Show children the clipboard you'll be bringing outside so you can draw pictures of the animals they find and write where they find them.

- Help children make predictions about what animals they might find outdoors, and where they might find them. As they share their predictions, record them in pictures and words.

Explore

Search for animals outdoors, in small groups or as a large group, for twenty to thirty minutes.

Encourage children to look carefully for animals outdoors.

- Suggest children use hand lenses, trowels, and field guides.

- Remind children of their predictions about what animals they might find and where they might find them.

- Model looking closely in a patch of weeds or under a pile of leaves.

- Suggest children explore spots that are likely to house small animals such as rotting logs or piles of leaves.

Observe and document.

As children explore and find animals, record observations and ideas. You might do the following:

- Take photograph and/or make sketches of the animals that children find and where the animals are found.

- Write down the questions children ask and snippets of the conversations they have that relate to their role as naturalists.

- Use the observation forms to record what children say and do.

Later, use the document annotation forms to highlight children's conversations and what is revealed about their inquiry skills and their understanding of habitats. (See sample below and drawing at right.) You will use this information to assess children's science learning. (See "Observation and Assessment" on p. 119).

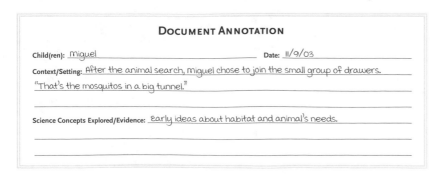

DOCUMENT ANNOTATION

Child(ren): miguel _____ Date: 11/9/03

Context/Setting: After the animal search, miguel chose to join the small group of drawers.
"That's the mosquitos in a big tunnel."

Science Concepts Explored/Evidence: Early ideas about habitat and animal's needs.

Reflect

Wonder about how habitats provide the things animals need in small group science talks for five to ten minutes.

EXAMPLE:

Our Predictions:

under the rocks we might find

centipede pill bug

EXAMPLE: We spent a lot of time talking about how to use the tools, and then we had lots of practice using them. And it paid off! Here's a picture of Sam carefully using a large trowel to dig up worms.

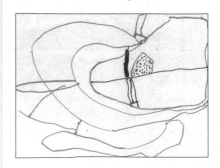

EXAMPLE: Miguel's drawing—"That's the mosquitoes in a big tunnel."

Review and share records.

After the animal search, sit indoors with a small group of children. Encourage them to tell one another about the animals they found and where they found them.

As children report on their findings, use a chart to draw and label the animals they found, and where they found them. Ask questions to probe children's thinking about how habitats provide for animals' needs. For example: "Why do you think the centipede lives under the log? The caterpillar on the tree?"

Engage children in a science talk about habitats.

After all interested children have had a chance to look for animals outdoors, gather the whole group together to share and examine their theories about how habitats meet animals' needs. Responses will reflect children's naïve ideas, which is fine. Your follow-up questions can help them examine their ideas more closely. For example: If a child suggests that worms like to live in the dirt because they like it there, ask the child to think about what it is about the dirt that worms like or need.

Share a chart from a small group discussion that you have with children after an outdoor search for animals. Initiate a conversation by asking questions such as, "Why would a pill bug want to live under a rotting log? A worm in dirt? An ant in a hole?"

Step 2: Make a Home for Visiting Animals

Children enjoy bringing animals indoors as short-term visitors. When they construct a new terrarium for visiting animals, children have a chance to learn through doing. At the same time, you are providing them with opportunities to think more deeply about the ways habitats have what animals need.

CORE EXPERIENCES

☐ Create a new terrarium.

☐ Collect animals.

☐ Review the process of constructing the terrarium.

☐ Think about how the terrarium helps to keep the animals alive and healthy.

PREPARATION

The focused explorations that follow this step develop from observations children make of animals temporarily housed in well-provisioned terrariums. Children often think more deeply about characteristics and behaviors of animals when they compare two different kinds. Therefore, we encourage you to repeat this step with a second animal. In the teaching plan we have chosen worms and snails as the examples;

you will need to adapt the plan to the animal you choose, although the main steps will remain the same.

The short-term visiting animals you bring into the classroom need to be safe to handle, large enough and slow enough to observe easily, hearty enough to live in a well-maintained terrarium, and plentiful enough so children can collect six to twelve of any one species. Check your local environment for animals that meet these criteria. Possibilities include worms, snails, slugs, pill bugs, and most caterpillars and beetles. If your local area does not support these kinds of animals, purchase some from a catalog (see p. 130). Make sure you receive six or more of the same kind of animal so children can observe variations within species. Each kind of animal you bring into the classroom as a short-term visitor will likely need its own unique terrarium. Animals can be housed together only when their habitats and needs are very similar.

Check the area where children will be exploring for broken glass, poison ivy, and so on. (See the safety guidelines on pp. 121–122.)

☐ Set up a small table with materials for constructing the new terrarium.

☐ Set up a second table with collage materials that children can use to represent the terrarium.

☐ Display photos and books that feature images of thoughtfully constructed animal terraria.

☐ Invite a guest naturalist to visit the classroom. (See extensions on pp. 110–111.)

SCHEDULE

Day One

☐ 5–10 minutes for a discussion to plan for the making of an animal terrarium

☐ 20–30 minutes for the whole group to collect items outdoors, or longer if you are taking small groups outdoors, one at a time

☐ 10–15 minutes for a meeting with the whole group to assemble terrarium

Day Two

☐ 5–10 minutes for a meeting before outdoor exploration

☐ 30 minutes for outdoor exploration to gather animals

☐ 5–10 minutes for a meeting with the whole group to talk about how to take care of the terrarium and what makes a good environment for the animals

Remainder of the Week

☐ 45–60 minutes for choice time so children can observe and represent the terrarium

☐ 10–15 minutes for a science talk

MATERIALS

- ☐ Reference materials about terrarium building (See pp. 135–136.)
- ☐ Empty container that can serve as a terrarium
- ☐ Charcoal, soil, water mister, and so on (See pp. 123–124 for a complete list of materials needed.)
- ☐ Trowels, science probes, plastic containers, and small insect nets
- ☐ Newspaper and whisk broom for keeping tables and floors clean
- ☐ Collage materials (yarn; pieces of Styrofoam and foam; paper in different colors, textures, and weights; glue; and oak tag or cardboard)
- ☐ Markers, paper, crayons, and colored pencils
- ☐ Sketchpad and pencil
- ☐ Camera, if possible
- ☐ Classroom terrarium from the open exploration
- ☐ Terrarium instructions (See pp. 123–125.)
- ☐ Copies of the observation record form (p. 143) and the document annotation form (p. 144)
- ☐ Chart labeled "Our Terrarium"

FAMILY CONNECTION

- ☐ Host a family evening so adults can experience the process of building a terrarium.
- ☐ During family meetings or through newsletters, explain the current classroom focus on respect for living things. Suggest families carefully catch and release the bugs they might typically kill at home, especially when their children are present.
- ☐ Provide families with the information they need to create terrariums at home. Remind them that these animals should only be kept indoors for a few days at a time, and that they need to be returned to the places they were found.

TEACHING PLAN

ENGAGE

Introduce constructing an animal terrarium in a whole group discussion for five to ten minutes.

Reflect on ways the classroom terrarium meets plants' and animals' needs.

You might ask the following:

- *What animals do we have in our terrarium now?*
- *How did we make this a good home for them?*
- *Why did we do that?*
- *What have we done to take care of them?*

TEACHER NOTE: I read Anne Mazer's book, "Salamander Room," to the whole group. It is the story of a little boy who made his room into a habitat for a salamander, which connected beautifully to our discussion of our terrarium and how it meets our animals' needs. There is so much in this book. I will read it again tomorrow.

EXAMPLE: I hung this chart near the vivarium and was surprised when Michale and Melissa recognized the words *water* and *pinecone*. So they're learning about how to make a vivarium (terrarium for small animals)—and they're learning about literacy too!

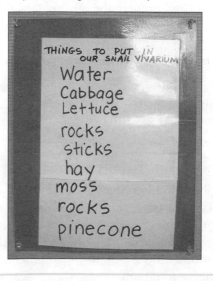

THINGS TO PUT IN OUR SNAIL VIVARIUM
Water
Cabbage
Lettuce
rocks
sticks
hay
moss
rocks
pinecone

Display the empty container you will use for the children's new animal terrarium. Explain that together you will use the container to construct a new classroom terrarium using materials from the outdoors, and that you will keep some worms or snails (or beetles, ants, spiders, centipedes, or caterpillars—whatever you have decided) in the terrarium for a week or two.

Make a list of items.

Help children make a list of items that might go in the terrarium. Help them think about what they will need to put into an empty terrarium to make it a place snails or worms can live. Ask the following questions:

- *If we want to keep snails (or worms) alive in our classroom, what do you think we will need to put into this terrarium?*

- *Why do you think we need to put in the dirt? Do we need plants?*

- *Do we need something special just for the worms?*

- *Where can we get these things?*

Look at reference books.

Model using a reference book to learn more about constructing a terrarium for snails or worms. You might say the following:

- *This book can help us find out more about what we need to put in our terrarium. Look at these pictures. What do you think they tell us about what we need?*

- *Are those things different from what we already decided we'd put in the terrarium?*

- *Do we want to add anything new to our list of things to collect?*

EXPLORE

Construct a terrarium and collect animals.

Day One
Plan and prepare the terrarium in a whole group meeting for forty-five to sixty minutes.

Review the list of items needed for a terrarium.

Sit with the whole group and review with children what they want to collect for their terrarium and where they might find those items. You might say the following:

- *Let's look at our list again.*

- *Where should we look for moss?*

Show children the trowels and containers you will bring outdoors. They can be used to collect plants, leaves, sticks, rocks, dirt, and so on. Remind them of the number of items (or the amount of any one item) they will probably need. See the resources on pp. 125–127 for information about how many plants and animals should be put in a single terrarium.

ISSUE: *What should I do if a child suggests we add beds for our snails?*

RESPONSE: Children are likely to talk about needs in terms of their own, which makes perfect sense. Instead of trying to "correct" children's legitimately held beliefs, you can probe the child's thinking. Ask: "What kind of a bed do you think a snail needs? How do snails sleep? What kind of sleeping place might a snail need? Why do you think so?" Then you might ask: "Have you ever seen a snail sleep?" Encourage the whole group to contribute their ideas.

EXAMPLE: As these boys looked for plants, they had this conversation:

Seth: *Let's get a plant for the terrarium. See, here's one.*

Jeff: *Be gentle, though.*

(Seth gently digs up the plant.)

Armin: *Look, you can see the roots.*

Assign pairs of children to collect certain things. For example: "Nina and Marcus, you two work together to dig up two small plants for our snails. Rose and Abigail, you two can dig up two plants also."

Collect terrarium materials.

Go outdoors either as a whole group or in small groups. Guide children as they carefully dig up a few small plants and collect dirt and a few small stones and sticks. Ask children to remind you how they think each item will help make the terrarium a good home for worms or snails.

Note: When you come back indoors, spray the items that need to stay moist—plants, moss, and soil. You can assemble the terrarium as soon as children come inside. If that's not possible, plan to have children assemble the terrarium the next day.

Construct the terrarium indoors.

Indoors, bring the whole group back together in a circle and set the empty terrarium and the items you plan to put in it, including those you purchased, on a tray in front of you. As each new item is placed into the terrarium, help children think about how it will help to keep their visiting animals alive and healthy. Ask the following questions:

- *You just put some decaying leaves into the terrarium. How will they help to keep worms alive?*

- *What is the purpose of dirt?*

If there is a second teacher in the classroom, ask her to use a chart to write down, in order, the ingredients you put into the terrarium. Next to each item on the list, write down the ideas children have about why each one is important for their animals' temporary home. Think aloud to give children information. For example: "I'm going to make sure this dirt isn't too packed down so it stays loose enough for roots to grow and so worms can crawl around."

Also, discuss which items are living and which are nonliving, or used to be alive. Some children may want to create their own chart, using a symbol to identify items as living, nonliving, or were once living.

Observe and document.

Document the process children go through to construct their animal terrarium and any thinking they might do about how it will meet their animals' needs.

- Photograph children adding materials to the terrarium, or make sketches of the items they add.

- Use the observation records to jot down the reasons children give for including each item—whether it is living, nonliving, or was once living—and how it will help meet their animals' needs.

Create a documentation panel.

Use your photographs, observational notes, and children's work to create a documentation panel that communicates children's ideas about how the terrarium helps to meet animals' needs. See guidelines for creating documentation panels on p. 142.

ISSUE: *Some of my children think rocks used to be alive. What should I tell them?*

RESPONSE: Try to understand their thinking by asking questions. For example, you might ask them, "What makes you say that?" or "When was it alive?" or "How was it different?" Later, conduct a large group science talk so children can share their different ideas. When children hear one another and have experiences with living things, they will develop new understandings.

EXAMPLE:

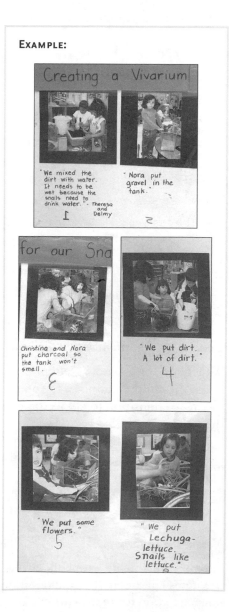

Creating a Vivarium

"We mixed the dirt with water. It needs to be wet because the snails need to drink water." – Theresa and Delmy   1

"Nora put gravel in the tank."   2

for our Sna

Christina and Nora put charcoal so the tank won't smell.   3

"We put dirt. A lot of dirt."   4

"We put some flowers."   5

"We put Lechuga-lettuce. Snails like lettuce."

Day Two
Collect and add animals to the terrarium for forty-five to sixty minutes.

Prepare to collect animals.

Sit with the whole class and remind children that you'll be going outdoors to collect worms or snails (or other animals you have identified) to bring inside to study, temporarily, while they live in the prepared terrarium.

Help children think about where they might look for worms or snails, and why they might look in those places. You might ask the following:

- *Where do you think we will find worms?*

- *How do you think our terrarium will meet their needs?*

Help children think about respectful ways to collect and transport animals. Show them the tools you'll be using (trowels; science probes; and small, empty plastic containers) and demonstrate how to use them.

Collect animals.

Outdoors, meet with your first small group and remind them that all the animals will be released in a week or two, and children will need to tell you where they found the animals so you can write the information down. That way, you all can make sure the animals will be returned to the places they were found.

As children find animals to bring indoors, help them think about ways the animals' needs are met by asking questions such as the following:

- *Why do you think the worms (snails) live here?*

- *What do you think they eat when they live here?*

- *Where do you think they go to feel safe?*

- *Does our terrarium have what the animals need? If not, what should we add?*

Add animals to terrarium within the hour.

When you come indoors, either bring the whole group together and invite the children to place the animals they've collected into the terrarium, or transition to choice time and work with small groups to do the same.

In either case, make sure the animals get into the terrarium within the hour. If children have collected more animals than their terrarium can support, make sure these extra animals are released back into their outdoor homes within the hour. (See pp. 125–127 for guidance on deciding how many animals can be housed in a single terrarium.)

Represent the terrarium.

Supply a small table with collage materials that look or feel similar to the items children put in the terrarium. For example, pieces of black foam are good for representing charcoal, sandpaper for dirt, felt for moss, and string for roots.

Issue: *I have a few children who are way too rough with the bugs and worms we find.*

Response: Ask children who are treating animals too roughly to remind you of ways animals should be treated. For example: "Show me how a naturalist uses the science probe to pick up the worm carefully." If necessary, assign other jobs, such as picking out stones, to children who are mishandling animals. Respect for living things is an important goal of this exploration.

Example:

On the following day at choice time, invite children to represent the terrarium. In addition to the collage materials, provide children with the following:

- Crayons, markers, paints, and colored pencils
- Photos or sketches of the experience

Engage children in conversation about their collages, drawings, or the photographs: "Tell me about this. Why did we add that?"

Later, use the document annotation forms to highlight children's drawings and words and what is revealed about their inquiry skills and their understanding of habitats.

REFLECT

Discuss how the terrarium provides for our animals' needs in a large group science talk for ten to fifteen minutes.

Focus the discussion.

Gather the children together in a group and put the terrarium in front of you. Use a documentation panel and/or children's collages to focus the discussion on the ways the terrarium meets the animals' needs. Focus the discussion with questions such as the following:

- *What can you remember about how we put the terrarium together?*
- *What things did we put in our terrarium? Why?*
- *What things in the terrarium help keep the snails moist but not too wet? What things do they eat? How do they keep safe?*

Discuss care of the animals' terrarium.

Help children recognize the ways they can take care of the terrarium by asking questions such as the following:

- *What do we need to do now to take care of the plants and animals in our terrarium?*
- *How can we make "rain" inside the terrarium? Would a water mister serve this purpose?*
- *What might we need to add? Decaying leaves? Fresh leaves?*

Create a list of things you will do to take care of the animals and plants in the terrarium. Post it nearby.

Step 3: Observe Animals Up Close

The children have created a home that can meet animals' needs. Now, they will be able to observe the animals closely, focusing on their different body parts and their behaviors. The goal of the animal study is to help children understand how animals are adapted to their environments and the many ways their bodies and behaviors allow them to eat, reproduce, and keep safe. Learning the names of body parts and exactly what they do is not as important.

> **REMINDER**
>
> Repeat step 2 if possible, building a terrarium for and collecting another kind of animal to compare to the first.

You might have some animals in the classroom that will go through different stages of the life cycle. This is an opportunity to talk with children about the life cycle itself—birth, growth and development, metamorphosis, reproduction, and death.

CORE EXPERIENCES

- ☐ Practice careful handling of worms or snails.
- ☐ Observe worms or snails up close.
- ☐ Use hand lenses and other magnifying tools.
- ☐ Create observational drawings.
- ☐ Represent animals' body parts and behaviors through movement.
- ☐ Talk about how children's bodies and behaviors are the same and different from those of the animals.

PREPARATION

SCHEDULE

- ☐ Enough time during choice time, over a number of days, so all children can spend time observing the animals more than once
- ☐ 10–15 minutes for a science talk

MATERIALS

- ☐ 6 hand lenses and other magnifying tools (such as large loupes)
- ☐ 6 shallow, clear plastic food containers or pieces of Plexiglas
- ☐ Spray bottle with water
- ☐ Different kinds of markers or colored pencils
- ☐ Black fine-tip felt markers
- ☐ Drawing paper and other materials for representation (See suggestions for long-term representation projects on p. 137.)
- ☐ Empty animal terrarium (See essential information on pp. 123–125 for guidelines.)
- ☐ Camera, if possible
- ☐ Copies of the observation record form (p. 143) and the document annotation form (p. 144)

FAMILY CONNECTIONS

Suggest families and children explore together in their neighborhoods, stopping to notice the animals that live around their homes. Encourage them to talk about the animals' needs and how they are met.

TEACHING PLAN

ENGAGE

Plan for careful observation of worms or snails with small groups.

EXAMPLE: This kind of discussion helps children become better observers. At the same time, these discussions provide a wonderful way for children to enhance their language skills as well.

> **Liza:** *It has lines.*
>
> **Sara:** *There's a purple line going through its back.*
>
> **Liza:** *It has stripes.*
>
> **Ben:** *It's like a snake.*
>
> **Teacher:** *How is it like a snake?*
>
> **Ben:** *It wiggles.*

Discuss respectful ways to treat the animals.

Sit with small groups of children during choice times. Remind them that the animals are visitors that need care. Support children as they take animals out of the terrarium by doing the following:

- Ask children to show you how they can carefully remove worms or snails from the terrarium and put them in clear plastic containers or on pieces of Plexiglas.

- Supervise water mister use.

- Comment on the careful behaviors you notice. Say something such as, "I noticed how carefully you dug for that worm!" or "You are moving the container nice and slowly!"

Also help children find respectful ways to handle the worms and to put them back in the terrarium.

EXPLORE

Observe animals during choice times until all interested children have participated.

Encourage children to look closely.

You might gently put a worm or snail on the table, on a piece of Plexiglas, or in a clear plastic container. Ask children what they notice. Encourage descriptive language by asking questions like:

- *What do you notice about this worm?*

- *What is it doing?*

- *What colors do you see?*

- *What can you see from underneath?*

Invite children to use a hand lens to look more closely. Show children photographs of worms or snails and encourage them to compare the animals in the photos to the live ones.

Invite children to compare themselves to the animals.

Use strategies like these:

- *Pretend your finger is a worm and wiggle it through the dirt. How does the dirt feel?*

- *Pretend you're a worm and wiggle on the floor as if you're moving across the Plexiglas. How does the Plexiglas feel?*

Introduce children to observational drawing.

Use this naturalist's tool by doing the following:

- Show children the paper, thin black "science pens," markers, or colored pencils that are available for making observational drawings.

- Invite children to choose a drawing tool that will help them draw a picture of the worm or snail when it is right in front of them.

EXAMPLE: We've been looking really closely at snails—what they look like and what their different parts are called. Now kids are beginning to capture the details they notice in their drawings. In this picture, Ena, age five, used spirals to show the shape of the snail. The three snails at the bottom of the picture with the dotted "antennae-eyes" focus more on the overall snail with all of its different parts. Jonathan, age three and a half, captures the snail's body shape and its antennae.

"I made the shell first because the shell is much bigger than the small small snail. Then i did the antenna-eye" Ena 5.2.00

"Do you see the snail?"

Jonathan

Engage children in conversation when they've finished their drawing. For example, you might ask a child to show you parts of the animal that correspond to parts of her drawing. Help children refine their drawings by saying something such as the following:

- *Which worm did you draw? Wow! That's a fat one! How can you make the worm you drew look fat like the real worm?*

- *How can you make your picture of the snail's shell the same color as the real one?*

Observe and document children's observations, questions, and ideas.

Use the observation record forms for the following:

- Jot down what children notice as they observe animals, and what excites them. For example: "Hank was really taken with the snail's antennae. He noticed that the antennae pull back when they're touched!"

- Note what children notice about how snails or worms can look different from one another.

- Note any questions children generate as they observe the worms and snails. For example: "Do snails leave slime wherever they go?"

You will use this information to guide and deepen the focus on animals.

REFLECT

Share children's observations of worms and snails in a science talk for ten to fifteen minutes.

Conduct a large group science talk.

Gather your whole group together to share and talk about children's observational drawings of worms or snails. Invite children to share their close-up observations of worms or snails, and ask them to describe the animal they drew. Then probe their thinking with follow-up questions:

- *The worm is so long and skinny! What do you think it can do because it's so long and skinny?*

- *What do you think its shell is for?*

Encourage children to move like worms and snails.

Probe their thinking with the following questions:

- *Why do you think the worm stretches out like that?*

- *Why do you think the snail stretches out like that?*

- *What do you think it's doing when it moves its antennae around like that?*

- *What are some things worms can do that you can't do?*

- *What are some things you can do that snails can't do? Why do you think they can't do those things?*

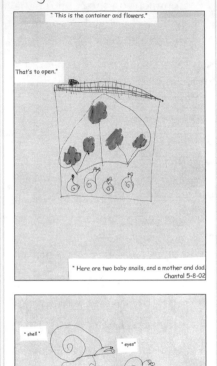

TEACHER NOTE: I'm keeping a chart at the snail table. When children are observing and questions come up, I write them down, along with the child's name. I need to plan some time in the next few days to follow up on some. I'll start with Chantal's ideas about what makes snails go into their shells, and how baby and adult snails differ.

" This is the container and flowers."

That's to open."

" Here are two baby snails, and a mother and dad.
Chantal 5-8-02

" shell "   "eyes"

" sticky stuff "

"I made a snail. This is his neck, his eyes and the stuff like his tummy. It's sticky and soft. It can stick to a lot of things. He sleeps inside his shell to get warm."
Chantal   5-8-02

Encourage children to share questions.

Help children think about and share the questions they have about worms or snails. For example, you might say the following:

- *I noticed Will looking at the different shapes the worms make. Will, what do you wonder about when you watch the worms make shapes?*

- *Rachel, when you hold a snail in your hand, what do you wonder about?*

Write down children's questions on a chart.

Close the meeting by recognizing ways children can pursue their questions. For example, you might say, "Let's see what we can learn by looking at our snails more closely, and let's see what our books tell us."

Reflect on children's list of questions.

Children's questions will fall into three general categories:

- Some of their questions can be answered through close observation. For example: "What will happen if we put the worm on the leaf? How does the snail move?"

- Other questions will need to be answered by books. For example: "Can snails smell? How do worms eat dirt?"

- And still others will invite children to theorize about why animals look and act the way they do. For example: "I wonder why a worm is so long. Are worms and snails like each other? In what ways?"

These questions are fun to pose as lunchtime conversation or as part of science talks.

Choose a question to focus your animal exploration.

The question should be answered through close observation of the animals in your classroom, and interest a number of the children.

Decide which of the topics the question addresses.

Topics could include the following:

- A body part (What are the snails' antennae for?)

- A behavior or movement (When snails or worms crawl to the end of the table, will they fall right off into our hands?)

- A life cycle (What is going to happen to the eggs our snails laid?)

Use the teacher's guide to help you facilitate a focused exploration.

- For an animal's body parts, see pp. 93–97.

- For an animal's behavior or movement, see pp. 97–100.

- For an animal's life cycle, see pp. 101–105.

Focus on Animals' Body Parts

Your children have been observing small animals up close and have undoubtedly been intrigued by animals' unusual bodies, which are so

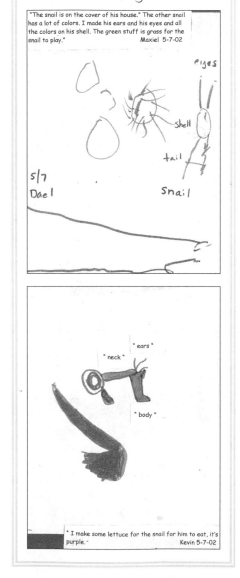

TEACHER NOTE: When Kevin and Dael were sharing their drawings, I realized they each referred to snails' ears. I wanted to help them find out more about snails' ears, but I didn't know if snails even had ears! I figured I'd find out, not because I want to just tell them the answer, but because I want to be prepared to guide their further inquiry.

"The snail is on the cover of his house." The other snail has a lot of colors. I made his ears and his eyes and all the colors on his shell. The green stuff is grass for the snail to play.   Maxiel 5-7-02

" I make some lettuce for the snail for him to eat, it's purple."   Kevin 5-7-02

When the children all focus on one question, they can share and discuss their ideas. However, small groups may be pursuing other questions if you can manage it.

different from their own. As you help children focus their observations, representations, research, and conversations on some of the animals' physical characteristics, you will provide them with opportunities to develop their understanding that animals' body parts have functions that help animals move, eat, avoid their predators, and have babies.

Core Experiences

☐ Focus observations on animals' unique body parts.

☐ Make observational drawings and models with a focus on an animal's particular body part.

☐ Use reference materials to learn more about an animal's particular body part and how it functions.

☐ Talk about how an animal's body part works to help the animal survive.

Preparation

Schedule

☐ 5–10 minutes before each choice time to make a connection from one day's exploration to the next

☐ 45 minutes or longer for choice time, three or more times a week, for as long as children seem interested

☐ 5–10 minutes for a science talk, once a week

Materials

☐ 6 naturalist kits

☐ Reference books that feature snails and worms

☐ 6 clipboards with paper

☐ Markers

☐ Clay or plasticine

☐ Collage materials that approximate snail's body parts

☐ Camera, if possible

☐ Copies of the observation record form (p. 143) and the document annotation form (p. 144)

☐ Chart labeled "Antennae"

Family Connections

☐ Send home notes periodically about what children are doing and learning.

☐ Encourage family members to join you to observe the animals, or read to children about the animals during choice times.

☐ Invite families to take care of the animal terrarium over a weekend or vacation.

The plans that follow focus on snails' antennae. You may want to choose a different focus based on your children's interests. For example: a mealworm's legs or a ladybug's shell.

TEACHING PLAN

ENGAGE

Use children's interests to focus the exploration in a whole group meeting for five to ten minutes.

Focus the observation.

Gather your children together in a circle and focus their thinking on snails' antennae. Help children share what they've noticed about snails' antennae. For example:

- *How many of you saw the snails' antennae?*
- *What did the antennae look like? What was the snail doing with them?*
- *How are the antennae alike? How are they different?*
- *What do you think the snails use their antennae for?*

Write their ideas down on the "Antennae" chart.

Prepare for focused observation.

Prepare children for their focused observations of an animal's body part. You might show children the naturalist kits. Remind them they can use the following:

- Clipboards and markers to draw snails and their antennae
- Field guides to learn more about snails
- Hand lenses and penlights to help them look very closely at the snail and its body parts

EXPLORE

Observe and represent antennae.

Encourage children to look closely at the animals' body parts.

During choice time, sit with a small group of children and observe snails. Encourage children to look carefully and closely at the snails' antennae by using the following strategies:

- Invite children to use hand lenses.
- Show them drawings or photos of snails and their antennae.
- Make your own close observations of snails' antennae.
- *What do you think the snails are doing with their antennae?*
- *When do the antennae go in? When do they come out?*
- *Why do you think antennae do that?*
- *How do the shorter antennae move? The longer ones?*

Encourage children to represent their observations.

Engage them in conversation about their work.

- Ask children to show you how the antennae move: "I noticed

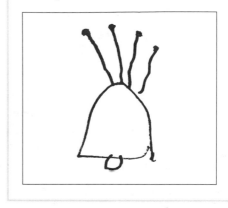

EXAMPLE: I started the discussing by asking Cathryn to show her drawing. She seemed most interested in the antennae, so she made four!

ISSUE: *When children went to observe snails today, they found a dead one. What should I do?*

RESPONSE: Take the children's lead; listen to their concerns and ideas. They might want to develop a class ritual—a way of dealing with death. Some ideas include writing a class story, reading a special book, planting a flowering plant, and burying the animal and marking the grave. Raising the question of why they think it died will encourage them to think about life cycles and give you the opportunity to find out some of their explanations.

EXAMPLE: Jonathan just turned three and a half. He pointed to the antennae on the live snail, then to the ones on his drawing and smiled! Then he felt the top of his head. "No antennae!" he laughed.

that you pulled your arms down to show how the antennae can pull back."

- Invite children to use the observational drawing materials to illustrate snails with antennae in and out: "The antennae you drew have these dots on the tops. Tell me about those dots."

- Invite children to use collage materials to make a model of a snail with the antennae out or in: "Tell me about your snail. How did you know where to put the antennae?"

Later, use the document annotation forms to highlight children's representations and words and what is revealed about their inquiry skills and their understanding of the characteristics and needs of living things.

Observe and document children's experiences, observations, and ideas.

An important aspect to look for is children's ideas about how snails use their antennae:

- Photograph children using their bodies to represent how snails use their antennae.

- Jot down the important parts of conversations you have with children, such as what they notice about how snails use their antennae and ideas they might have about why snails need their antennae.

Create a documentation panel.

Use your photographs and observational notes, as well as children's work to create a documentation panel that shows children observing animals closely. Include their drawings and words to communicate to families and other teachers some of the children's ideas about the animals' unique body parts and how they are used. You will use the panel to focus children's thinking during the upcoming science talk.

REFLECT

Share theories about the purpose of antennae in a whole group science talk for ten to fifteen minutes.

Help children share what they have learned about snails' antennae.

Use your documentation panel as well as children's observational drawings to help children share what they've found out about snails' antennae. Ask questions like these:

- *What did you find out about the snails' antennae?*
- *Up close, what do antennae look like?*
- *Can you use your body to show me how antennae move?*

Invite children to think about how antennae are used.

Read the "Antennae" chart aloud to the group and ask them if they would like to change or add anything. Use questions such as these to probe children's thinking:

EXAMPLE: This teacher did not reject Amelia's comments. Rather, she encouraged her, and others, to share their ideas and the observations on which they based their theories.

Amelia: *They use their antennae for kissing. I saw them.*

Teacher: *Tell us about what you saw.*

Amelia: *Two snails—their antennae touched.*

Teacher: *How did you know it was a kiss?*

Amelia: *It looked like one.*

Teacher: *What do you think, Billy? You were watching too.*

REMINDER

This focus provided an example of how you can support children's interest in one body part. You can do the same with other body parts as long as children are interested. For example, children might want to focus on worms' bodies or snails' mouths.

- *What do you think snails use their antennae for? What makes you think that?*
- *How does that help the snail?*
- *Why do you think we don't have antennae?*
- *Why do you think worms don't have antennae?*

Use a different color marker to add to or revise the chart, highlighting children's latest thinking.

Focus on Animal Behavior

Children delight in observing and wondering about animals and their behaviors—how they move, how they eat, and how they protect themselves. As children observe, they are likely to ask lots of questions. You can help children pursue their questions by providing them with opportunities to observe their animals closely over time, think about the animals' needs, and compare the animals to other animals, including themselves!

CORE EXPERIENCES

☐ Focus observations on animals' behavior.

☐ Represent animals' behaviors with their own bodies, in observational drawings, and through models.

☐ Use reference materials to learn more about an animal's behavior and how it helps it survive.

☐ Describe animals' behaviors and discuss how those behaviors help them survive.

PREPARATION

SCHEDULE

☐ 5–10 minutes for a meeting before each choice time

☐ 45 minutes or longer for choice time, three or more times a week, for as long as children remain interested

☐ 10–15 minutes for a science talk, once a week

MATERIALS

☐ 6 naturalist kits

☐ 6 clipboards with paper

☐ Markers

☐ Clay and plasticine

☐ Collage materials such as yarn and strips of foam

☐ Camera, if possible

☐ Copies of the observation record form (p. 143) and the document annotation form (p. 144)

FAMILY CONNECTIONS

☐ Send home an invitation for family members who keep or raise animals to come into the classroom and talk to the children about how they care for their animals.

☐ Invite families to care for the worms over a weekend or during vacations.

TEACHING PLAN

ENGAGE

Share observations and interests in worm movements for five to ten minutes in a whole group meeting.

Focus the upcoming observation.

Gather your group together and help them remember some of their worm observations:

- *We have been putting worms on the table, and we have been watching them very closely. What have you noticed the worms doing?*
- *Show me with your arm how it wiggled! Was that the only way the worm moved?*
- *What did you notice about its head. Its tail?*

Prepare children for focused observations of animal behavior.

You might show children the naturalist kits. Remind them they can also use the following:

- Clipboards and markers to draw worms
- String to track the worm's trail
- Field guides to learn more about worms
- Hand lenses and penlights to help them look very closely at the worms and how they move

Ask children how they will focus on worm's movement:

- *How are you going to look even more closely at how worms move?*
- *What do you think you'll see them doing?*
- *How can we learn more about how worms move?* (For example: books, videos, and so on.)

EXPLORE

Observe and represent the ways worms move during choice time for up to forty-five minutes, as long as children are interested.

Encourage children to look closely at the animal's behaviors.

Sit with children at a small table during choice time, and encourage them to look closely at and talk about the worms' movement. You can try the following:

> The following plans focus on how worms move. You may want to choose a different focus based on your children's interests. For example: how a snail eats or how a pill bug protects itself.

- Invite children to use hand lenses to look at worms and string to track their path.
- Have books available that feature photos, drawings, and information about the animals children are observing.

To focus children's observations and thinking on the worms' movement, ask questions such as the following:

- *Let's look very closely! How does the worm move without legs and feet?*
- *What parts of the worm help it move?*
- *How do you think the worm goes under the dirt?*
- *I wonder why the worm keeps stretching out so long.*

To focus children's observations and thinking on worm behavior, ask questions such as the following:

- *I wonder why the worm is moving so much.*
- *Why do you think that worm is moving away from the puddle?*

Encourage children to represent their observations.

Provide time and materials for children to represent their observations, and encourage them to use different methods:

- Observational drawing—Encourage children to use lines or arrows to show how the worms move.
- Movement and drama—Encourage children to move like worms do on the floor.
- Collage and model making—Encourage children to make models of worms using clay, wire, and collage materials that approximate worms' bodies and movement, such as yarn and strips of foam.

Display children's drawings on a bulletin board and their models on a shelf. Label each representation with children's descriptive language about their piece.

Observe and document children's ideas.

An important aspect to look for is children's ideas about how or why worms move the way they do. Use the observation record form to jot down the important parts of conversations you have with children about the following:

- How worms move
- Ideas about why worms might move like that

You might also photograph children moving like worms. You will use these records to guide the upcoming science talk.

REFLECT

Discuss how worms move and why they move in that way in a science talk with a small or large group for ten to fifteen minutes.

Try to move the conversation from description to ideas about how animal movement and behavior are related to meeting their needs. Questions that begin with "Why do you think . . ." or "I wonder . . ." encourage children to develop and express their ideas.

EXAMPLE: Marian is one of the youngest children in the class. She made this drawing to illustrate a worm's movement.

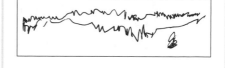

EXAMPLE: Alexa is interested in how and where her snail moves. I am struck by the lines she used to capture its movement.

REMINDER

This step provides an example of how you can support children's interest in one type of animal behavior. You can do the same with other animal behaviors as long as children are interested.

Help children share their observations.

Bring a group together to share and discuss their observations of how worms move. Focus the discussion using one or more of the following:

- Ask for a few volunteers to show the group how to move as worms do.

- Invite children to share their observational drawings, collages, or models with the group.
  - *Tell us about your work. What did you do to make it look like a wiggling worm?*

- Recount a conversation you heard between children about their worms and how they move.
  - *Dan said his worm sticks its head out when it moves, and Ally said hers slips along on slime. What do you think, Maggie?*

- Help children share their observations by asking questions such as the following:
  - *We enjoyed watching you move like a worm! What did you do to look like a moving worm?*
  - *Your drawing of the fat worm has these arrows next to it. What do they mean?*
  - *I was at the naturalist table yesterday, and I heard Mark and Alice talking about the moving worms. Mark said it moves with slime, and Alice said, "No, it moves with tiny feet." What do the rest of you think? How could we find out?*

Encourage children to share their ideas and theories.

Invite children to share their ideas about why worms move as they do. For example, why do they stretch long and then get small, wiggle and burrow, make shapes, and climb over pencils? Expect children to create theories that are based on their life experiences. Do not worry if they are not "correct." For example, they might theorize that worms wiggle because they're ticklish. You can help them examine their theories with questions such as these:

- *Why do you think worms move in the way they do?*

- *Where do worms live?*

- *How would it help a worm to move in the way it does?*

Help children examine their theories even further with follow-up questions. For example, if a child suggests that worms stretch and wiggle to go fast, ask them why they think worms might need to move quickly.

Record children's ideas about why worms move in the ways they do on a chart. Identify children's ideas with their names. For example: "Rose thinks worms stretch their necks out because they are trying to look around to see if anything's coming to eat them."

Example: This teacher built on the children's interest in how snails move. This conversation will help to draw other kids in and further focus their explorations, while helping children reflect on what they've observed.

> **Teacher:** *Some of us were looking at the snails today and we were talking about how it feels when they walk on our arms.*
>
> **Child 1:** *Yeah, it tickles.*
>
> **Child 2:** *It's sticky.*
>
> **Teacher:** *It tickles and it's sticky. Remember when we looked at the book that said snails have one big foot, but it doesn't walk with its foot like we do? So I'm wondering how it moves.*
>
> **Child 2:** *With his slime. He pushes.*
>
> **Child 1:** *With its tail.*
>
> **Child 2:** *He moves slowly like this (child demonstrates with his fingers how slowly the snail moves).*
>
> **Teacher:** *I'm going to write this down—how the snail moves—because that's something we're going to be talking about.*

Example: Summaries like this one help children reflect on what they have learned over time.

How Do Snails Move?
Ena: They make slime from the bottom part.
Delmy: They move their whole bodies like a muscle.
Christina: They wiggle their tails and push their bodies.
Theresa: They walk with three feet.
Joana: They go very slow.
John: They walk fast with lots of feet.

Focus on the Life Cycle

As part of their recent explorations, children may have observed baby worms, snail eggs, baby snails, or other evidence of birth. They have also most likely experienced the death of an insect, worm, or snail. Three- to five-year-olds rarely observe a complete life cycle, from birth to reproduction to death. They can, however, observe animals grow and develop over time. By inviting them to dramatize, represent, sequence, and discuss their observations, you will provide a foundation for later understanding of the life cycle. This teaching plan focuses on the painted lady butterfly. You will need to adapt it if you are studying a different life cycle.

CORE EXPERIENCES

☐ Observe the life cycle of one or more kinds of animals.

☐ Discuss how the animals change as they move through the life cycle.

☐ Compare life cycles of animals including themselves.

☐ Represent and dramatize stages of the life cycle.

PREPARATION

The metamorphosis of a painted lady butterfly is quite wonderful, but children can have experiences with this kind of change observing meal worms, tadpoles, and other butterflies. The plans that follow focus on the painted lady. During its life cycle, the painted lady changes from one form to a completely different form—from egg to larva to pupa to an adult butterfly that lays eggs and then dies. The goal of the this step is to help children observe and describe the life cycle. Learning the names of stages and exactly how they differ is not as important.

Observing different animals going through life changes can enhance children's experiences. If possible, bring animals other than painted ladies into the classroom to observe over time, such as mealworms and frogs. Mealworms and frogs go through metamorphosis too.

Children can also observe the life cycle by watching animals that do not go through metamorphosis. Land snail and guinea pig babies look like small versions of their parents when they are born. They do not go through metamorphosis.

If possible, let children observe two different kinds of animals, each with different life cycles: one that goes through metamorphosis and one that doesn't. That way they will have opportunities for comparing the two.

Depending on the animals you decide to bring into the classroom for observation, you will likely need to order them well ahead of time. See pp. 129–130 for information about ordering animals.

SCHEDULE

☐ 5–10 minutes for a meeting before each choice time

☐ 45 minutes or longer for choice time, a few times a week over the course of the animals' life cycles

☐ 10–15 minutes for a science talk, once a week

MATERIALS

- ☐ 6 naturalist kits
- ☐ 6 clipboards with paper
- ☐ Markers
- ☐ Clay or plasticine
- ☐ Collage materials such as pipe cleaners, tissue paper, foam packing peanuts, and so on
- ☐ Scientifically accurate picture books about the life cycles of the animals that children will be observing (See suggestions for books and media on p. 130.)
- ☐ Camera, if possible
- ☐ Copies of the observation record form (p. 143) and the document annotation form (p. 144)
- ☐ Make a chart labeled "Our Painted Ladies" (or the name of the animal your children are studying)

FAMILY CONNECTION

Encourage family members to join you in observing animal life cycles during choice times. Suggest that families take care of animals over a weekend or during vacations.

TEACHING PLAN

ENGAGE

Introduce the focus on life cycles for five to ten minutes in a meeting with the whole group.

Focus observations on life cycles.

Gather your group together and focus upcoming observations on life cycles. Begin by reading aloud from a scientifically accurate picture book about the life cycle of the animal children will be studying. Invite children to talk about the book and compare their own lives and experiences to what happens in the book.

Engage children in conversation:

- *How did the baby caterpillar grow?*
- *What about you? Do you grow like that?*
- *What happens to you when you grow?*

Introduce the new animal.

Introduce the painted lady caterpillars. Invite children to share their ideas about these animals.

- *What do you think these are? What makes you say that?*
- *What do they remind you of?*
- *How do you think we should take care of them?*
- *What do you think will happen to them as they grow?*

EXAMPLE:

OUR CATERPILLARS

* They'll eat each other.
* They'll turn into butterflies.
* They have babies.
* They get fat.

Record children's ideas in drawings and words on a chart labeled "Our Painted Ladies." Tell them that they will have opportunities to observe their caterpillars and how they grow during choice times at the naturalist table.

EXPLORE

Observe the caterpillars and record their growth and changes over time, during two or three choice times over the course of several weeks.

Prepare children for the exploration.

Before children's first observation of caterpillars, bring the group together and remind them of a few things:

- The caterpillars should not be handled.
- The naturalist tools are available for making close observations and observational drawings.
- The chart with children's ideas about how the caterpillars might grow and change will be posted next to the naturalist table so they can change or add to their ideas.

As children continue to observe over time, invite them to share with the group any recent observations. Encourage children to share observational drawings or models as a way of reminding everyone of the changes they have observed in their painted lady. Ask questions such as the following:

- *What do you think will happen next?*
- *Why do you think that?*
- *What do you think is helping the painted lady grow? Change?*

Invite children to observe animals as they pass through different stages of a life cycle.

During choice times, sit with a small group of children at the naturalist table. Encourage children to observe closely and to notice any changes.

- Pass out hand lenses.
- Wonder aloud if they will notice any changes in the painted ladies.
- Share books with illustrations of painted lady butterflies at different stages of their life cycle and ask children how their animals look the same or different.

Ask questions such as the following:

- *Antoine said he saw "white stringy stuff" next to two of the painted lady caterpillars. What do you think that white stringy stuff is? Where do you think it came from?*
- *What makes you think that?*
- *Maria says the chrysalis is wiggling. Has it always been wiggling? How do you know? Why might it wiggle?*

- If possible, take pictures of the stages of growth.
- If you do not have a camera, make sketches, and encourage children to do the same.
- Then use your photographs or drawings to make a documentation panel or class book so children can review the stages.

EXAMPLE:

Encourage children to represent their observations.

During choice times, as children observe changes in the painted ladies, encourage them to represent their observations by using one or more of the following methods:

- Dramatization
- Observational drawing
- Model making
- Collage
- Journals

Make connections between the children's work and the animals' changes by using questions and comments such as the following:

- *Tell me about these curved lines on your drawing. Which part of the painted lady are they?*
- *I noticed that you started wiggling just like the pupa did when you were the painted lady in its chrysalis.*

Use the document annotation forms to highlight children's representations and words and what they reveal about their inquiry skills and their understanding of the characteristics and needs of living things and the life cycle.

Observe and document children's observations.

It is important to look for children's ideas about how painted ladies move through their unique life cycle.

Use the observation record form to jot down the important parts of conversations you have with children about the following:

- How painted ladies grow and develop; for example:
  - 9/21/02 Nigel noticed that the chrysalis is changing color.
  - 5/04/03 Louis asked, "What happens to the chrysalis that never opens?"
- How painted ladies develop the way they do and how their needs are met during the unique life cycle

You might also take photos of children as they dramatize the life cycle.

Make a documentation panel.

Use your photographs and observational notes, as well as children's work, to create a documentation panel that highlights children's observations of the painted ladies' life cycle. (See p. 126 for guidance.) You will use the panel to focus children's thinking during the upcoming science talk, as described below.

REFLECT

Discuss how a painted lady caterpillar changes into a butterfly for ten to fifteen minutes during a science talk with the whole group.

> **TEACHER NOTE:** Some of my children were fascinated by the silk the caterpillars spin. They were trying to figure out the purpose of that silk. They thought a spider came in at night and spun it. I noticed today that the caterpillar was actually spinning what eventually became an anchor for the chrysalis. All the children watched, their eyes wide open. I really think that the best way for children to learn about the life cycle—to learn about anything—is through direct experience.

Engage children in a discussion.

Use your documentation panel and read from the chart, "Our Painted Ladies." Invite children to share their developing theories about the stages in a painted lady's life cycle. Questions like these will help focus the conversation:

- *What do you think happens to the caterpillar when it's in the chrysalis?*
- *What do you think a butterfly can do that caterpillars can't do?*
- *What do you think caterpillars can do that butterflies can't do?*

Record children's ideas about how painted lady caterpillars go through metamorphosis on the chart. Use a different color marker so children can see their most recent thinking.

Compare life cycles.

If your children have the opportunity to observe more than one kind of animal as it goes through the life cycle, help them compare the two by using their drawings, photographs, books, and bodies to dramatize the different ways animals grow.

- *Can you show me what a butterfly does when it comes out of its chrysalis?*
- *What do baby butterflies look like? What do baby snails look like?*
- *How are they different from adult butterflies (or snails)?*

Wrapping Up

Children have had many experiences using their senses and naturalist tools to observe plants and animals. They have dramatized, modeled, drawn, discussed, and read about plants and animals and their characteristics and needs. There are many ways you can help children reflect upon and celebrate their explorations. As children share their experiences with each other and with their families, they will gain a deeper understanding of the concepts and inquiry skills that have been central to their exploration.

CORE EXPERIENCES

☐ Plan ways to share naturalist exploration with families and friends.

☐ Host an open house.

PREPARATION

☐ Check with your staff and administration, and identify a date for hosting an hour-long open house to share children's experiences.

☐ Ask children to decorate invitations for families and friends.

☐ Collect the charts, documentation panels, graphs, class books, observational drawings, tree journals, models, and other documents the class created during "Discovering Nature." Display them, along with children's favorite nature books, around the classroom.

TEACHER NOTE: I read "The Very Hungry Caterpillar" to the class after our exploration of butterflies and caterpillars. The children loved the story and the beautiful artwork. They also loved being detectives—figuring out which details were inaccurate, then explaining how they knew.

TEACHER NOTE: The children in my class love to use the new big words they've learned recently! Today I heard the words "chrysalis" and "antenna," and I read a book that used "proboscis." I wonder if they'll use that one.

REMINDER

If children are interested, you and your class can examine the life cycles of other animals in similar ways.

Schedule

☐ 5–10 minutes for a planning meeting a few days before the open house, and again for about an hour before the open house

Materials:

☐ Make a guest book for family and friends to write their comments at the open house.

Teaching Plan

Engage

Introduce the open house in a meeting with the whole group for five to ten minutes.

Help children plan for the open house.

Gather your group together. Explain that you would like to plan an open house so they can share with their families and friends some of the things they've done and learned as young naturalists. Ask the children which nature discoveries they would like to share with their guests. Record their ideas, using words and pictures, on a chart.

Discuss the role of "host."

Help children anticipate what the open house will be like and how they can act as hosts. Together, list the many things children can do with their guests:

- Observe visiting animals.
- Look at the many plants growing indoors.
- Read or look through any of the field guides and other nature books.
- Look at documentation panels, class books, collages, journals, observational drawings, models, and so on.
- Make an observational drawing.

Involve children in helping you set up the classroom for the open house.

Conduct the Young Naturalists' Open House

As you welcome your guests, point out the guest book. Ask them to write a comment about what they do and see during the open house before they leave. Invite guests to make observational drawings of the plants or animals. Have children teach the guests how to use the naturalist kits. Invite guests to read with children.

The open house described in this step is only one way to bring closure to "Discovering Nature." You can also help children share and reflect on their experiences with nature by doing one or more of the following:

- Invite children to take turns bringing home and sharing any class books you've written while they were discovering nature.

- Videotape children acting out the life cycle of a painted lady butterfly. They could start as eggs, change to a caterpillar, and then turn to a butterfly that lays eggs and dies. Invite children to take turns bringing the video home to share.

- Display children's drawings and collages in the school's lobby.

- Post all of your documentation panels around the classroom and revisit a few each day during meetings with the whole class. Ask children what they remember about each experience.

Teacher note: Throughout our observations of painted lady caterpillars turning into butterflies, we had a video camera available to us. By the end, we had a nice, twenty-minute video that featured the butterflies and each of the children. So we decided to feature the video at our open house. You could tell parents were so proud as they watched their children—and the children were so proud of what they had learned!

extension activities

The focus of *Discovering Nature with Young Children* is on children's close observation of plants and animals in their environments. However, direct observation is not the only way children can learn about living things, their needs, or their characteristics. As children discover nature, they can explore these ideas in many ways.

As children explore, you can enrich and broaden their experiences and learning by taking trips, introducing them to other naturalists, and sharing relevant books and videos. The extension activities described below should not become substitutes for children's outdoor and indoor observations. Rather, they should complement these explorations.

We suggest that you do an extension activity about once a week during focused exploration.

Take a Field Trip

Visiting a new place allows children to explore different environments. It provides opportunities to compare and contrast the kinds of plants and animals found in new environments to those living in the classroom terrarium and in the outside areas you have been studying. Children can also see the ways plants and animals meet their needs in the new environment.

SUGGESTED DESTINATIONS

- Controlled indoor environments such as greenhouses and plant nurseries
- Natural outdoor environments such as wet woods, dry woods, ponds, and beaches

Preparation

- If you are going to visit a greenhouse, nursery, or museum, visit the site ahead of time. If possible, speak with the staff and discuss the purpose of your visit. Remind them that children ages three through five are active explorers: They need hands-on experiences, short presentations, and time to ask questions.

- If you are going to explore an outdoor area, visit the site ahead of time. Make sure it's a safe place for children to explore. Decide if you will be collecting living things on your trip. Consider bringing back some specimens to observe and study in the classroom. If you collect small animals, make plans for returning them to their environment of origin within a day or two. If you will be collecting during the visit, make plans for bringing and using appropriate equipment.

Before the Trip

- Decide how children will carry and use their naturalist kits at the site.

- Arrange for adult volunteers to join you on the trip. Plan a time to talk with them about what will happen on the trip, your expectations for what children might engage with, and the ways they can support children's observations at the site. (For example: show volunteers how to use your naturalist tools, and give them a list of questions they can ask to focus children's observations.)

- Consider alerting children to one part of the visit, such as a greenhouse full of flowers or a stream that empties into a pond. Suggest particulars they can look for (such as, "I wonder if there will be lily pads in the stream" or "I wonder if the greenhouse will be hot inside"). You may also consider identifying a couple of things to look for (such as the method for watering plants at the greenhouse or the types of flowers growing near the parking lot).

- While children will notice lots of things about the environment you choose to visit, you may want to provide a focus. You might ask the children a question or two and draw out their predictions, recording them in words and pictures. Possible questions include the following:
  - *How do you think the greenhouse/beach/wet woods will be different from our terrarium/park/playground?*
  - *What new plants and/or animals do you think we'll see? Will we see a lot of these new plants and/or animals at this place? Will all of them be the same?*

During the Trip

Assign small groups of children to each teacher and adult volunteer. Encourage children to act as naturalists. Invite them to do the following:

- Observe closely.

- Use hand lenses and penlights.
- Describe animals and plants (such as the number of caterpillars or pine trees).
- Record some observations by making drawings.
- Collect things, if appropriate.

Remind children of your questions or things to notice. Ask follow-up questions to probe their thinking. For example:

- *How is this greenhouse different from our terrarium?*
- *Where do you think the bugs are?*
- *What do you think they find to eat?*
- *What new plants do you see?*
- *What shape are their leaves?*
- *Which plants have bark that's different from what we've seen before?*

Document what children do, say, and see so you can help them discuss and reflect on the visit later in the classroom. If you have a camera, take pictures of the children making their observations.

AFTER THE TRIP

Have a brief conversation about what you saw. Ask questions such as the following:

- *What did you like best about the visit?*
- *What did you see? Hear? Smell?*
- *What was special about the place we visited?*

Put out drawing and art materials. Encourage children to represent their trip. Write down excerpts from their stories.

The next day, or when your photos have been developed, use children's observational drawings, videotapes, audiotapes, and/or photos and documentation panels as reflection tools to discuss the question you focused children's observations on during the visit. Probe children's reflective thinking with questions such as the following:

- *What did you notice about this plant? Animal?*
- *How do you think that helps it meet its needs?*
- *How is it the same as the ones we have in our terrarium? How is it different?*
- *What do you think the animal eats? What makes you say that?*
- *Do you think the plant will ever flower? What makes you think that?*
- *How was the swamp/beach/greenhouse different from our park?*
- *Do you think our snails could live there? What makes you think that?*

Record children's ideas, in drawings and words, on a chart.

Invite Guest Naturalists into the Classroom

Children's interest is piqued by visitors. When you introduce children to an adult who integrates the skills, practices, and knowledge of naturalists into their work and recreation, you provide them with a powerful role model as well as an immediate resource.

PREPARATION

- Send home a letter asking family members if they, or anyone they know, would be available to share an expertise, hobby, or interest related to the young naturalist exploration.

- Talk with the naturalist ahead of time and describe the kinds of explorations your children have been doing, their interests, and their questions. Suggest the naturalist bring any tools she uses to show the children. Ask if she minds being videotaped.

SUGGESTED GUESTS

- A naturalist

- Someone from the Audubon Society

- Someone from a local extension service, including the 4-H organizations

- A scientist who studies plants (*botanist*) or one that studies bugs (*entomologist*)

- A horticulturist or someone who runs a greenhouse or plant nursery

- A gardener

- Someone who raises animals

- A bird-watcher

- A landscape architect

BEFORE THE VISIT

Have a brief conversation with your class about what your visitor does, and ask children what they might want to learn from their guest. Write down children's questions to share with the visitor. The children may want to know more personal things such as where they live or if they have children. These questions are also important to children because they help them see the visitors as real people who use science inquiry in their daily lives.

DURING THE VISIT

Ask the visitors to talk about what they do, and invite them to share journals, tools, books, and stories related to their work as you refer to children's questions. Give children a chance to ask additional questions. Share the terrarium, children's observational drawings, and classroom books. Ask for comments and suggestions for further study.

AFTER THE VISIT

Have a brief conversation with your class. Ask children what they learned from the visitor and refer to the video of the visit, if one was made. During choice time on the following day, invite children to join you at a small table to draw pictures about the naturalist's visit for a class book. Ask children about their drawings and write their words down.

Use Books and Videos to Extend the Exploration

There are endless numbers of books and videos that deal with themes from nature. Some entertain, some inform, some inspire. The books that inform a naturalist's study need to be scientifically accurate, engaging, and informative for young children. As children move in and out of open and focused explorations, teachers can offer resources in a variety of ways to support the inquiry.

BOOKS

- Books should be integral to children's work and play, and they need to be accessible. Stories, photos, diagrams, poems, lists, and informative text each offer something unique to the process. Make a special effort to display books that have engaging pictures related to the plants and animals children have been observing. Encourage children to visit the book corner to look through these books, and encourage other adults to read to small groups or individual children.

- Recommended books to use with extension activities appear in "Books and Videos" (p. 130). Use the guidelines presented below and in the section on books and videos to help you choose an assortment of books. In addition to having library books around the classroom, you can use different kinds of books for extension activities in different ways.

FICTION

- Fact and fantasy
- Real-life

Choose books that present or raise questions about plants' and animals' needs, the ways living things meet those needs, or the unique characteristics of living things. Then, when you read aloud each book to an individual child, a small group, or the whole group, you'll be providing a new opportunity for children to wonder about the book's setting, learn vocabulary, and focus their thinking on young naturalist concepts without disturbing the flow of the story. You might raise issues or ask questions, such as the following:

- *What did the duck find to eat?*

- *Where did the turtle go to feel safe?*

- *How did the little girl feel about being so close to a squirrel?*

NONFICTION

- Field guides—Take field guides outdoors and show children how guides name plants and animals and sometimes tell a little about their characteristics.

- Information books—Use information books with small groups during choice time as you observe plants and animals more closely.

- Image books—Use image books with a few children at a time, so everyone can see. Read aloud or summarize short pieces of text in response to children's interests and questions. Ask children how the plants or animals in the images compare to the living things they've been observing:
  - *How does this snail look like the one you were just observing?*
  - *Before we read what the book says, why do you think pill bugs curl up like you've seen them do?*

Preview a variety of these kinds of books (see "Books and Videos," p. 130, for more information) and choose ones that have clear images of the kinds of plants and animals children have actually been observing, as well as others they can use to compare to what they've been seeing.

BIOGRAPHY

As you read naturalist biographies aloud, look for opportunities to discuss the characters' love of nature, their respect for living things, and the ways they use tools, observations, and resources as a naturalist. You may ask questions such as the following:

- *What do you think the naturalist was really interested in?*

- *What did he see?*

- *What questions did she ask?*

- *How did he take care of the environment?*

POETRY

Poets share their feelings about nature, images, and sounds. Use poets' words to help children experience the feelings and see the images they paint with words. Read aloud a variety of poems and ask questions that help children connect their experiences to those expressed in the poetry, such as the following:

- *That poem was about grasshoppers. What words did the poet use that reminded you of our grasshoppers?*

- *What words would you add?*

VIDEOS

- Videos that stimulate children's exploration and raise questions for them can be integrated into their work and play. Use the guidelines presented on p. 130 to preview an assortment of videos. In short, they should be scientifically accurate, not too complicated, engaging, and without advertisements.

- Preview videos and choose pieces that feature the kinds of plants and animals children have been observing, or ones they can easily compare to those in the local environment. View an excerpt or two with children. If the audio track is too sophisticated or unrelated to your exploration, mute it and focus children on the images. Ask questions that help children wonder about what they're viewing. Encourage them to compare the images to their own experiences.

- Play a video more than once. We often see different things a second or third or fourth time.

resources

Science Teaching

YOUNG CHILDREN'S INQUIRY

"Young Children's Inquiry" is a framework to help you think about how new knowledge is created in science. (See the chart on the following page.) It is useful whether you think about the inquiry of a scientist, your own inquiry, or the inquiry of a child. The framework suggests that the stages follow one another. To some extent they do, but the many arrows suggest that the process of inquiry is not linear, and children will move back and forth and around as they explore the world around them.

Inquiry is about questions, but it's hard for children to ask questions about something if they haven't had a chance to get to know the thing or the materials or the event, whether it is balls rolling, snails, or water flow. So the first stage in the framework is to *engage, notice, wonder, and question*—it is a time for children to play, to see what they already know, to mess about in a rich environment with little direct guidance or structure. As children explore, they ask questions through words or actions. As they continue, they may be struck by a particular idea or question such as "I wonder what would happen if I put this block here?" or "Why is the snail on the wall?"

Many of the questions children raise may not be ones that are possible or interesting to investigate. "Why is the sky blue?" cannot be explored directly. "What is the name of this plant?" will not go far. But "What are ways I can get the water to move?" is the start of a rich investigation. At this stage, children often need adult guidance to begin to *focus observations and clarify questions*. They need to be encouraged to make some predictions and guesses about what might happen.

When children engage in more focused explorations, they are entering the experimental phase of inquiry. Even very young children, given the right materials and teacher support and guidance, can *plan, predict, and take action; observe closely; collect, record, and represent experiences and data; reflect on experience; explore patterns and relationships; and construct reasonable explanations and ask new questions.* Notice that on the framework, this process goes around and around. Children may explore a question for a long time. Their explorations may lead to new questions and new investigations.

When children have a good deal of experience and begin to form some ideas, they need to be encouraged to step back from the investigative work, review and reflect on what they have done, and *share, discuss, and reflect with the group,* as well as formulate ideas and theories. By sharing, children have opportunities to reflect and relate their ideas and experiences to what others have done. Differences in experience may demand a return to the exploration. New questions may come up leading to new explorations.

THE TEACHER'S ROLE

Teachers play a number of major roles when exploring science with children. This section includes such responsibilities as the following.

INQUIRY

Engage, notice, wonder, question

Focus observations, clarify questions

Plan, predict,
take action

Ask new
questions

Explore, investigate

Observe
closely

Reflect on experience,
explore patterns and
relationships, construct
reasonable explanations

Collect, record, represent
experiences and data

**Share, discuss, and reflect with group;
draw conclusions; formulate ideas
and theories**

- Create a science-rich environment
- Engage children in science explorations
- Focus and deepen children's experiences and thinking

Observing and assessing, which is also important, will be described in the next section.

CREATE A SCIENCE-RICH ENVIRONMENT

One of the most important roles you play in this exploration is creating an environment and culture that supports and encourages children as young naturalists—your classroom must convey the excitement and wonder of observing and learning about living things. Giving children multiple opportunities to explore plants and animals in the outdoor environment is critical, so children can explore living things in their natural habitats. You can also create a science-rich environment in your own classroom. Placing growing plants and terraria around the classroom allows children opportunities to observe and think about plants and animals. Displaying interesting field guides, picture books, and information books about the plants and animals they have been observing allows children to learn more about the living things they have seen.

Organizing and placing tools (such as hand lenses and penlights) and materials for representation (such as markers, paper, clipboards, and clay) so children have easy access to them and can return them independently will encourage ongoing observation and representation. Charts, documentation panels, children's drawings, and posters of living things displayed at children's eye level helps children build on previous explorations, while sparking new ones. Check your environment periodically to see what changes are needed to make your environment reflect the progress of the exploration. For example, are there new tools to add? Which children's work samples and documentation panels should be put away, and which should be added? Which new books reflect children's current interests about the natural world and could enrich their experiences?

Children also need time to explore. You may need to adjust your classroom schedule so children can explore living things in their natural habitats and in the indoor terrarium several times a week over time. Also be sure to schedule a science talk with the whole class at least once a week so children can share their observations and ideas, and learn from the experiences of others. You will also need to develop a few, simple classroom rules for keeping children and the plants and animals safe. (For more information about creating a science-rich environment, see "Getting Ready" on pp. 16–19 and the "Classroom Environment Checklist" on p. 139.)

ENGAGE CHILDREN IN SCIENCE EXPLORATIONS

WHAT CHILDREN ARE DOING: As children move into the open exploration, some will be immediately excited by the ideas and challenges. Others will be more reluctant, perhaps observing a plant or animal for a minute or so before moving onto another activity. Still others will prefer to play on the swings or choose a different activity.

TEACHER ROLE: Spend time with those children who are ready to look for and observe living things. Do not push those who are not engaged. Some will be drawn in by your enthusiasm and the excitement of their peers. You might partner children who are excited about the exploration with children who are less engaged. For example, you might say, "Teresa, can you show Ben that plant you found? Could you both find another one just like it?" You might also try to incorporate science into children's play. For example, you might ask children in the block corner to build a home for ants, or you might add toy trees to the sand table. Try sharing some good naturalist books as well. Reading a book about a small creature might draw some children into the exploration. (See "Books and Videos" on p. 130.)

When children explore plants and animals, sit with them and observe. Children who are deeply involved with their work are best left to do so. You need to observe and take note. Through their actions you get clues about what problem they may be trying to solve and what questions they may be asking. These observations will help you guide later discussions and reflection. If children are ready to talk and listen, you might describe what children are doing and seeing. For instance, "You used the trowel really carefully to dig up the plant. Wow, look how long its roots are!" Also encourage children to share their observations in words and actions, such as using words or their bodies to describe the shape of a leaf. Do not correct children's ideas. Rather, use words, pictures, drawings, and more direct experiences to encourage children to consider their ideas in new ways. By bringing in resources and offering new experiences, children can explore and refine their ideas.

FOCUS AND DEEPEN CHILDREN'S EXPERIENCES AND THINKING

As children pursue their exploration of living things, you will have many opportunities to push their thinking and their ideas. These opportunities will arise as children engage in conversations, as children represent and document their work, as you use resources, and as you document children's ideas and experiences.

Conversations

As children explore living things, listen to their conversations with each other, and talk with them informally and during weekly discussions with a large group about their experiences, observations, and ideas.

Communication with Other Children

WHAT CHILDREN ARE DOING: As children work side by side, their conversations with one another push them to put words to their actions and communicate some of their thinking. Their questions of one another may challenge and extend what they are doing and intrigue them with new wonderings. Their debates and arguments will push them to think more about their own ideas and those of others.

TEACHER ROLE: Children's conversations are likely to be very different from those guided by an adult. They are likely to be more directly tied to their fantasies, rules of the game, and requests for help. Your role is to listen carefully and document what may be useful for later discussions and reflection.

Discussions with Children

WHAT CHILDREN ARE DOING: As children are engaged in their work they may welcome interactions with the adults around them. Discussion can raise new questions and suggest new investigations, while helping them to develop their abilities to communicate about their work and thought.

TEACHER ROLE: Engaging children in conversation as they work must be done carefully and only after spending some time observing them. Children should not be interrupted unless they want to talk, and conversations should be about what they are doing and thinking. Good questions to get started include descriptive ones: "Can you tell me about what you are doing? Where did you find that leaf? What else did you find? What did the worm you found look like? What shape was it? What size? How did it feel when you touched

it?" Further discussion can probe more deeply and focus on science concepts. "Why do you think the leaf fell off? How do you know that the worm eats dirt? How could we find out if the worm likes other things?"

Science Talks

WHAT CHILDREN ARE DOING: During science talks, children share their experiences and their thinking; listen to those of others; and try to make connections between what they have been doing, what others have been doing, and what they already know. It also is a time for children to struggle with new ideas and theories as old ways of understanding are challenged by new experiences.

TEACHER ROLE: Science talks are a critical part of science teaching and learning, helping children to communicate and reflect on their experiences and ideas and to focus their thinking on the science concepts and processes. Your role is to draw out children's ideas and experiences and to challenge their thinking. During your discussions, maintain a focus on the process and substance while encouraging children to tell and dramatize their stories. Use children's representations, your own documentation, and books as a springboard for these discussions: "Here's a picture of the plant you observed. Can you tell us about it?" "Here's a picture of the worm you found. Can you use your body to show us how it moved?" Further discussion can probe more deeply, helping children to compare and reflect on their observations and ideas: "How are your bean plants alike and different?" "Will thinks the mealworms move with their feet. Dara says she thinks they hop like frogs. Maxine, what do you think? How do you know?"

Discussions with a small group are easier to manage than large groups, but the science talks with a large group are important as well, so that children can hear about the ideas and experiences of many others. Begin slowly; start with five- to ten-minute science talks with a large group and increase the time as children's engagement increases. Be sure that all children who want to contribute have a chance to do so. Provide physical props to support children who are less verbal and use your records to support those who are reluctant to speak out. For example, you might display a clay figure of a turtle a child made and say, "Kerry, tell us about your turtle. Can you point to the turtle's parts?" Such discussions may encourage children to try new things and question their thinking.

Representation and Documentation

WHAT CHILDREN ARE DOING: When children document or represent their work in various media, they think about their experiences in new ways. Drawing a picture of the worm in his naturalist's notebook will often prompt a child to observe more closely and highlight details. Or using their bodies to show how a snail moves can help children think more deeply about the animal's characteristics and behaviors.

TEACHER ROLE: It is critical for you to make available materials for children's documentation and representation and to provide space for work and display. But your role goes beyond making available materials. You will need to encourage children to document and represent their work on a regular basis, even if some are reluctant. You may do this by working with them, having them work in pairs, providing notebooks, and celebrating what gets done. Children's documentation and representation also may be the focus of individual or group discussions. Ask a child to describe her work; invite children to use their work in class discussions; probe children's thinking by asking them to tell you why they did something a particular way. "Tell me about your drawing. I noticed you drew this long line here. Where is that part on the plant? What are you trying to show?" "I noticed you drew the root. So what do you think the root is for? How does it help the plant live?" "This is a great question you have in your notebook. How might we go about answering it?"

Using Resources

WHAT CHILDREN ARE DOING: Children learn about the natural world through close observation of plants and animals in their environments. However, direct observation of the familiar is not the only way children can learn about living things, their needs, and their characteristics. They can also deepen their thinking by using books, talking with experts, and going on field trips.

TEACHER ROLE: Use resources—such as books, field trips, and guest experts—to enrich explorations of living things. Be sure to display books that have engaging pictures about the plants and animals children have been observing, so children can compare the illustrations to their own observations. Field trips to a greenhouse, a nature preserve, beach, and so on encourage children to compare and contrast the plants and animals in these new environments to those they have observed. Guest experts can provide new information about plants and animals, which can lead to new questions and investigations.

Document Children's Ideas and Experiences

WHAT CHILDREN ARE DOING: As children engage in their explorations, they are certainly thinking about many things. Their actions are the outward reflection of those thoughts. Observing and documenting what children do and say can help you understand their ideas and questions. While young children have many ideas, they tend to focus on the present. Without support they may see experiences as somewhat isolated events and are not always aware of the development of an idea, an experience, or a project. It is also difficult for them to record and keep track of all the data they are gathering. The products of ongoing documentation can be used to provide many opportunities for children to revisit the process and progress of their work and reflect on their understanding.

TEACHER ROLE: Your role is to be the documenter. You can document children's work and the data they are gathering from their exploration in many ways— videotape and audiotape; anecdotal records; photographs; and lists of predictions, observations, and questions. You can then use this documentation to help children revisit, build on, and reflect on their data, ideas, and observations. For example, by going over your notes about children's questions, you will be able to guide them in reflecting on what they found out over time and the ideas they have developed about certain living things. Or by reviewing charts about the living things children found and where they found them, you can help children think about habitats and animals' needs. Documentation panels play a significant role in children's science explorations. It is your role to create a sequence of photos, sketches, science-related conversations, lists of predictions and observations, or children's work with brief annotations that allow children to "replay" and reflect upon what they have done and what has happened. Use the panels as a springboard for stimulating discussions, reenactments, and further explorations. (See "Guidelines for Creating Documentation Panels" on p. 142 for more information.)

Observation and Assessment

Observation, documentation, and assessment are critical steps *throughout* the exploration, helping you gain a picture of children's growing skills and understanding of living things. What children say and do will provide you with important clues about children's understanding of the characteristics, needs, and behaviors of living things; their science inquiry skills (such as their ability to explore, collect data, and so on); and the question they may be asking. Your analysis will help you determine the next steps to take with individual children and the group as a whole. You can also share information about children's science learning with families, your program or school, and funders.

THREE KEY ELEMENTS OF ASSESSMENT

1. Collecting data. Spend at least ten minutes three times a week collecting different kinds of data that captures children's level of engagement and their science understandings. This data can include the following:

   • Written observations that capture what children say and do and wonder about as they explore living things

   • Photographs, videotapes, and audiotapes that capture children's action and words

   • Samples of children's work that illustrate each child's growing abilities (such as observational drawings, dictated stories or poems, and two- or three-dimensional collage representations of plants or animals)

2. Analyzing data regularly. Time spent reflecting on your collection of documents will help you understand the growing skills and understandings of each child in your class. The more kinds of documents you have, the fuller picture you will have of each individual. Examine varied documents reflecting the work of each child, and look across the class to gain a picture of how the group is developing.

3. Drawing conclusions and making decisions. Analysis of the documents you have collected will help you make the important connections between your teaching and the children's learning. Use your analysis of children's growth to consider what your next steps should be with individual children and the group. Who needs encourage-

ment in order to become fully engaged in the explorations? Who is ready for a more complex challenge? Who needs help finding a voice for their observations and ideas? This will be an ongoing process that informs your teaching, helping you refine your approach to teaching science.

A TOOL FOR SCIENCE LEARNING

"Science Outcomes: Science Inquiry Skills and Science Concepts" (pp. 147–148) will tell you what to look for as you analyze your data. This overview of learning goals is organized in two sections: science inquiry skills and science content. For each outcome, it provides three child behaviors sequenced from less to more experienced. These behaviors illustrate how a child might demonstrate their skill or understanding. Use these outcomes and behaviors to help you focus children's science learning and to assess their growth.

TOOLS FOR COLLECTING AND ORGANIZING YOUR DATA

The following three tools will help you document children's inquiry skills and growing understanding of the science concepts.

1. Observation Record. This form provides a structure and format for recording your observations of children's naturalist explorations. Place copies of the form strategically around the room and bring them outdoors so you can jot down your observations throughout the day. Use the observation and documentation section of each step of the teaching plan to focus on science concepts and inquiry outcomes as you complete the form. See the sample form on the next page.

2. Document Annotations. Use this form to annotate photos, work samples, transcripts, or any other documents that you may have. When filling out the form, highlight what the document reveals about children's inquiry skills and their understanding of science concepts. Then attach your annotation to each document. The time you take to identify the significant science in each document will help you when it comes time to analyze children's growth and draw conclusions about your teaching. See the sample on the next page.

3. Learning Record. This record provides a format for collecting and analyzing the information you have collected about each child. Note that the

content and inquiry items are the same as on the chart "Science Outcomes: Science Inquiry Skills and Science Concepts." Begin a learning record for each child as soon as you start to review your collected observations and documents. Note the evidence you have from observations, conversations, and work samples. Use dates to reference specific documents. Add to the records regularly. Your goal is to have a statement about each outcome for each child by the end of the exploration. Note where the gaps in information are and plan to focus on engaging those children. At the end of the exploration, check the appropriate box in the child growth column. See the sample on the next page.

Make copies of the assessment forms that are included in the appendices and use them to document the growth of children in your classroom.

Essential Information

SAFETY

Exploring the outdoors is very important to the development of young children's ideas about the world around them. As with all experiences with young children, considerations must be made for their safety. The area you explore with children should be as free of hazards as possible, such as rusting metal and broken

OBSERVATION RECORD

Children's Names	Seen and Heard
Yvonne	• Looks at birds in the tree and watches them fly away • Blows seeds from milkweed pod and turns to catch them
Kevin	• Sees a spider's web in tall grass and watches it move in the wind • Asks, "Where's the spider?"

DOCUMENT ANNOTATION

Child(ren): Ken   Date: 4/12/00

Context/Setting: Ken had been observing crickets in the terrarium over several choice times. He was reluctant to draw at first, but he was inspired when he finally noticed the cricket eating. He was excited to share what he had observed and learned about crickets.

Science Concepts Explored/Evidence: Characteristics of living things, showing several body parts for the cricket and petals on the flowers that are the food. He is also beginning to understand the needs of living things, as shown in his representation of the food.

LEARNING RECORD

Child: Hannah

Science Inquiry Skills	Child Growth	Evidence
Engages, notices, wonders, questions	☐ Emerging ☐ Sometimes ☒ Consistently	9/23 Looked in compost and under slide for centipede 10/12 Collected nine different kinds of leaves
Explores, investigates	☐ Emerging ☐ Sometimes ☒ Consistently	10/2 Turned Plexiglas over to make sure snail was stuck 11/10 Looks for acorns under all the oak trees
Collects data	☐ Emerging ☒ Sometimes ☐ Consistently	9/30 Counts six snails in terrarium 11/13 Notices oak and maple leaves have different shapes

glass. You may feel you are not personally able to recognize potentially harmful plants and animals. In general, a little knowledge will help you to feel more comfortable about exploring the outdoors. Here are a few suggestions to help you along your way.

ANIMALS

In most settings, there is little concern about the animals children will encounter. It is vital to be aware of serious allergies (such as bee stings), but most of the other small animals to be found outside the classroom door will be harmless. It will be important to contact your town's health department to learn whether there are local health concerns.

PLANTS

Of all the troublesome plants, you are most likely to run into poison ivy or poison oak, depending on where in the country you live. Once you know what these plants look like, it will be much easier to anticipate any potential problems from them. A number of Web sites offer clear pictures of plants, how to cope with them, and information on other plants that might be worth knowing more about. See the resource section about books and Web sites for teachers (p. 135) for several examples.

CREATING AN OPEN COMPOST HEAP

A compost heap is essentially a pile of materials that were once alive (organic) such as leaves, twigs, branches, grass clippings, or weeds. Given time, these organic materials attract small (both visible and microscopic) animals that will eat and digest them. After the material has been eaten and digested, what remains is called *compost*. The main goal of this compost heap will be to attract small animals for the children to observe and explore. The directions that follow are for an open compost heap.

MATERIALS

- An outdoor space approximately 3 by 3 feet (Look for a quiet, less-traveled part of the playground—an area bordered by a fence or wall can work well. This space should be on dirt or soil, *not* on concrete or asphalt.)

- Organic material such as fallen leaves or grass clippings (If you use grass clippings, they should not come from lawns that have used pesticides or herbicides. These chemicals can kill the animals you are hoping to attract.)

Note: If leaves are not available, you can use a large piece of wood (approximately 2 by 2 feet) as a "bug board."

INSTRUCTIONS

1. Locate a quiet spot for the compost heap, about 3 by 3 feet, near the school.

2. At least two weeks before you plan to begin the exploration, place a pile of organic material (such as leaves, weeds, twigs, or grass clippings) at the site located in step 1. If no leaves or other organic materials are available, you can use a large piece of wood, or "bug board," instead. This will not really decompose but should attract small animals.

3. Moisten the pile of organic material or the area around the piece of wood liberally.

4. During the two weeks that follow try to be sure that the pile of organic material remains moist. Check the bottom of the pile or under the wood from time to time for signs of life.

CONSTRUCTING A TERRARIUM

The construction of several different kinds of terraria is required.

MAKING A TERRARIUM FOR LOCAL ANIMAL VISITORS

Long-Term Visitors

Materials

- A large, clear container with a fine mesh (small holes) cover. The container should hold at least five gallons and be about 15 by 8 by 10 inches. Possibilities for containers include the following:
  - Purchased plastic terraria (see "Where to Purchase Materials," p. 129)
  - Plastic storage boxes (such as those available at most department stores)
  - Old fish tanks (even if they leak)

- Covers for your containers (It will be important that the covers have holes small enough to prevent small animals, such as insects, from escaping into your classroom. Possibilities for covers, available at most hardware stores, include cheesecloth and flexible, fine-mesh screening material.)

- Large rubber bands or tape (to secure cover)

- Gravel, pebbles, or sand (for drainage)

- Charcoal granules

- A digging tool, such as a hand trowel or small shovel

- A spray bottle with water (for keeping the soil moist)

Instructions

1. Find a nearby site where you will be able to dig up a small area of soil, plants, and even bugs. Look for as much variety of life as possible.

2. Find a location in your classroom where you'll be able to keep your terrarium. It should not be in direct sunlight for long periods of time, nor should it be in the dark or near a heat source.

3. Put a small amount (about one inch) of the gravel, pebbles, or sand at the bottom of your container.

4. Spread a layer of charcoal granules on top of the gravel.

5. Bring the terrarium with the gravel and charcoal outside. Dig soil from the area you have chosen and place a layer two to three inches deep on top of the layers of gravel and charcoal. Dig up a few small plants, taking care to dig as much of the soil around the plants' root systems as possible. Retain as much of the root system as you can. Possible plants include grass, moss, tree seedlings, and weeds.

6. Plant the plants carefully and add any other materials you find such as dead leaves, small rocks, and so on. Your goal is to make the terrarium look as much like the outdoor area as possible.

7. Add water to keep the soil evenly moist. If you can, mist the leaves of the plants.

8. Cover the container, being careful that the cover does not bend any tall plants too much.

9. Bring the terrarium back to your classroom. You will need to maintain the moisture level in the terrarium throughout the long-term visitors' stay.

Short-Term Visitors

During focused exploration you will be housing animal visitors in your classroom for about one week at a time. The terrarium you construct for these visitors need not be large or elaborate. It must, however, include enough material from the visitor's habitat to ensure its survival for the duration of its visit.

Materials

- Clear containers (such as one- or two-liter plastic soda bottles with the tops cut off or clear plastic deli containers)

- Covers for your containers (It will be important that the covers have holes small enough to prevent small animals, such as insects, from escaping into your classroom. Possibilities for covers, available at most hardware stores, include cheesecloth and flexible, fine-mesh screening material.)

- Large rubber bands or tape (to secure cover)

- Gravel, pebbles, or sand (for drainage)

- Gardening charcoal, optional (to filter out impurities)

- A digging tool, such as a hand trowel or small shovel

- A spray bottle with water (for keeping the soil moist)

Note: You should prepare and establish the plants and soil portion of the terrarium before you add animals.

Instructions

1. Put a small amount (about one inch) of gravel, pebbles, or sand at the bottom of your container.

2. Dig up enough plant material to fit comfortably into the container you are using for the terrarium. Take care to include as much soil and roots from the plants as possible.

3. Place the plants and soil in the container.

4. Add water to keep the soil evenly moist.

5. Take children out into your schoolyard or local park with empty plastic containers and covers. Collect small animals (such as worms, snails, or caterpillars) and put them in the containers. Add the animals to the terrarium when you return to your classroom.

6. After about a week of observation, return the animals to where you found them.

Very Short-Term Visitors

When children explore the outdoors there is likely to come a time when you will find a need to have a container ready in case of a particularly exciting or unusual find. Most often this will involve wanting to bring something indoors to look at it more closely, and then release it in a day or two. It is not necessary in this situation to prepare an elaborate habitat, as many animals can survive away from their habitat for a very short period, especially if they have access to

water. If you have a few containers in a variety of sizes nearby, one can be called into use with short notice.

Materials

- Clear containers with covers

  Possibilities for containers include the following:
  - Clear, plastic supermarket cookie containers
  - Purchased plastic terraria (see "Where to Purchase Materials," p. 129)

  Possibilities for covers include the following (available at most hardware stores):
  - Cheesecloth
  - Flexible, fine-mesh screening material secured with tape or rubber bands
  - Plastic wrap with a few small holes

Instructions

1. If you anticipate finding and bringing back an interesting short-term visitor, bring along one or two extra containers with lids when you and the children go out to explore.

2. When you find an interesting visitor, carefully collect it and place it in the clear container you have brought for this purpose.

3. Add a few materials that will support the visitor's survival for the next day or two, such as the leaf you found it on or other materials you found near it.

4. Cover the container, being sure there are several air holes in the cover.

5. Bring the container and visitor back to the classroom. Place it in a location out of the direct sunlight, or the container may heat up dramatically.

6. After a day or two of observation, return the visitor to where you found it.

MAKING A TERRARIUM FOR NONLOCAL ANIMAL VISITORS

At some point you might purchase an animal (such as the suggested animals that appear in this section) from a pet store or from a biological supply company. In most cases, you will have the opportunity to purchase a ready-made habitat for this animal for an additional cost. Or, you might choose to construct a habitat for this animal on your own. The materials you will need for this terrarium will, of course, depend on the particular animal and its needs. Some animals need dry and warm conditions; others need moist habitats; and so forth. It will be up to you to research the needs of your particular animal and provide adequate housing for it (see "Finding and Caring for Animals," below). You must check with the store or company about what to do when the visit is over. Many animals you purchase may not be local to your area and should not be released.

FINDING AND CARING FOR ANIMALS

Note: Generally, once you have finished with your animals, you should not release them outside unless that is where you first found them. Most small animals purchased from reputable biological supply houses are accompanied by instructions for environmentally safe release or disposal at the end of your exploration.

Among the best classroom pets are mealworms, earthworms, land snails, and painted lady butterflies. They are easy to care for, reasonably easy to get, easy to handle (some more than others), and endlessly fascinating for children.

MEALWORMS

Mealworms are available at any pet store, since they are used as food for other small animals. They often come in two sizes, regular and large. We suggest the regular size. Because mealworms live in dried grain (such as oats, bran, and so on), they are not an appropriate choice for the kind of terrarium suggested in "Making a Terrarium for Local Animal Visitors" (p. 123). Mealworms survive easily in a small container of dried oats or wheat bran, with a small piece of potato, apple, or carrot for moisture.

Mealworms undergo a four-stage life cycle in a relatively short period of time. Generally, this change, or *metamorphosis*, will occur more quickly in a warmer climate than in a cooler one. Mealworms begin as eggs, then become larvae (the "mealworm" stage), then become pupae (similar to a butterfly's chrysalis), and then become adult brown or black beetles. The adults mate, lay eggs, and eventually die. As mealworms grow and change they shed their skin many times. In a mealworm colony that has been going for several months you are likely to find mealworms in all stages of development (including dead adults) along with shed skin. The eggs are very difficult to see, but once they hatch you will begin to notice very small mealworms that become easier to spot as they grow. Meal-

worms are easier to handle, easier to care for, and less expensive than butterflies.

Caring for Mealworms

1. Buy twenty to fifty mealworms at a local pet store. If you can only buy them in quantities of 100 or more, that is fine too.

2. Place them in a small plastic container, such as a deli or yogurt container or small plastic terrarium—the clearer the better.

3. Poke a few holes in the cover of the container.

4. Put about two inches of dried oats or wheat bran in the container.

5. Put a small (½ x ½ inch) piece of potato, apple, or carrot in the container, and cover.

6. Check the mealworms from time to time. Open up the container to take the mealworms out, observe them, check on any changes, and see whether or not the oats have begun to grow mold. If you notice any mold, replace the oats immediately. Add more oats periodically as the supply dwindles.

If you decide not to keep your mealworms indefinitely, they can be used as fishing bait. If you must destroy them, they can be frozen for an hour and then thrown away.

EARTHWORMS

Earthworms can be found in most places that have rich, moist soil. They are especially fond of piles of moist, composting leaves or other organic material. They can also be purchased at stores that sell bait or through any number of companies that specialize in composting. Or, purchase them through any of the biological supply houses mentioned on pp. 129–130.

Caring for Earthworms

1. Find a plastic or Styrofoam container with a lid.

2. Fill it about halfway with soil.

3. Place the earthworms on the soil.

4. Cover with a layer of organic material, such as grass clippings, leaves, or lettuce.

5. Place another layer of soil on top.

6. Moisten the soil, but do not make it wet.

7. Place the cover on the container.

8. Poke some holes in the cover and on the side of the container near the top.

9. Place the container where it will not get direct sunlight.

10. Open up the container from time to time to dig for the worms. Be sure the soil has remained moist but not wet. One way to determine the moisture level is to squeeze a small amount of soil. It should remain in a ball shape without drops of water coming out of it.

When you are finished, the earthworms can be used in a compost heap or simply released where they were found.

LAND SNAILS

Land snails can be found in many backyards and gardens, usually in dark, moist areas where they try to avoid the sun's drying rays. If you cannot find them easily near you, you can order live snails from Connecticut Valley Biological Supply Company (see p. 130). There may be restrictions for sending snails to some locations. Land snails will need plenty of regular moisture and a diet of plant material supplemented with calcium in order to stay healthy. If you purchase land snails or if you plan to collect them outdoors, you can care for them by following these instructions.

Caring for Land Snails

1. Find a clear plastic container with a lid. Poke holes in the lid small enough that the snails can't escape.

2. Place a layer (about half an inch) of gravel or sand on the bottom of the container for drainage.

3. Add a layer of soil (about four inches).

4. Place a few small plants (such as grass, moss, or seedlings) in the soil, ensuring that there is room for the roots.

5. Add one or two small rocks and a stick or twig.

6. Make sure the soil is evenly moist. Spray the plants and sides of the container with water.

7. Place the snails in the container.

8. Provide them with two or three small pieces of green leafy vegetables (not iceberg lettuce) and a piece of chalk.

9. Watch the snails closely over the next few days to see if they are eating anything. Be careful that the vegetables do not begin to rot—once they begin to wilt, replace them immediately.

10. If you have found the snails outdoors, be certain to return them where you found them after their visit. If you have purchased them, enjoy them forever! Over time, you are likely to find eggs and then a new generation of snails.

PAINTED LADY BUTTERFLIES

Painted lady butterflies are wonderful to observe. However, they cannot be handled by children and must be released two to three days after becoming adults. Painted lady starter kits can be purchased from the sources listed on pp. 129–130. Monarch and other varieties of butterflies may be found locally as eggs or caterpillars. They too can be cared for temporarily in the classroom and then released as adult butterflies.

Each of the four distinct life phases of a painted lady or other butterfly is a natural part of the life cycle. A butterfly mates, lays eggs, and dies. The egg soon hatches into a larva which is an immature animal. The larva of a butterfly, the caterpillar, looks completely different from the adult. The larva eats and grows. Soon, the larva enters into the pupa stage. A chrysalis is the pupa of a moth or butterfly. During the pupa stage, change takes place. When ready, the fully developed butterfly comes out of the pupa. The mature adult is now ready to reproduce and continue its life cycle. The process of making the changes from one stage to the next is called metamorphosis.

Caring for Painted Lady Butterflies

Simply follow the instructions that accompany the kit. If you have collected eggs or caterpillars locally, be sure to bring in the plant material on or near which they were found, and release the adult butterflies soon after they have emerged from the pupae.

OTHER POPULAR CLASSROOM ANIMALS

The following are popular classroom pets that generally require more attention than the animals mentioned above. With care, however, they offer interesting opportunities for brief classroom exploration. Some must be purchased, others can be found near school playgrounds throughout much of the United States. A particularly useful reference for caring for small pets is *Pets*

in a Jar: Collecting and Caring for Small Wild Animals, by
Seymour Simon (Puffin Books, 1988).

Check "Resource Books and Web Sites for Teachers"
(p. 135) for other helpful references.

- Water snails are easy to care for in an aquarium,
but unlike land snails, they are often difficult to
look at closely. They can be collected from a
healthy pond by scooping out some of the sedi-
ment at the bottom along with the water.

- Pill bugs (also called roly-polies) and sow bugs
can be found in moist locations, such as under
logs or outdoor planters. They actually have gills,
so they need to be kept in moisture, but not under
water. They look similar, but pill bugs actually roll
into a ball when threatened, and sow bugs do not.

- Crickets are available at most pet stores, but they
are difficult to maintain for long periods of time.
They can be kept in a cage with a moistened
sponge for water and a small piece of cut-up potato or apple.

- Madagascar hissing cockroaches are very large
and frightening to some people, but they are really quite tame, especially if handled frequently.
Although they do best in warmer environments,
they make excellent classroom pets. However,
not many teachers feel comfortable keeping
them. They can be kept in a small covered plastic
container with a thin layer of wood shavings
(such as hamster bedding). They will need a constant supply of water. They eat all kinds of fruit,
but seem to do especially well with dog biscuits.

- Fish are perennial favorites, but they and the
equipment they frequently need require constant
attention.

- Reptiles, such as skinks, chameleons, and anoles
(small reptiles that turn from green to brown or
vice versa depending on the need for camouflage),
require a constant warm temperature, which is difficult to assure in many parts of the United States.
Extra equipment, including some sort of heating
element and lighting, will be required twenty-four
hours a day where there is cold weather.

Many other commonly found small animals such as
ants, ant lions, tadpoles, fireflies, and ladybugs can be
brought inside for brief visits of up to a week. See
"Very Short-Term Visitors" (p. 124) for how to collect
and care for these special visitors.

GROWING AND CARING FOR PLANTS

BEAN SEEDS

Although almost any kind of seeds, including corn,
radish, pea, and pumpkin, can be germinated in a
classroom, we suggest bean seeds for the following
qualities:

- Large enough to handle
- Easy to find
- Easy to see
- Relatively fast-growing

*Note: You must use dried beans, which can be found in most
supermarkets. Look for whole beans, such as kidney, pinto,
black-eyed peas, or lima beans. Split peas will not germinate.
Also, be aware that packets of seeds intended for gardening are
usually treated with a fungicide, so are not appropriate for use
with young children. Be sure to check labels; those that have
not been treated will say so on the packet.*

Planting in Soil

Materials

- Bean seeds (three or four per container)
- Containers (such as small plastic cups with two or
three holes poked in the bottom for drainage, or
plastic planting pots)
- Potting soil

Instructions

1. Fill the containers about three-quarters full with
potting soil.
2. Place the bean seeds on the soil surface keeping
them as separate from each other as possible.
3. With your index finger, push each seed into the
soil until the first joint of your finger is level with
the surface of the soil.
4. Cover the seeds with soil.
5. Water until all of the soil in the cup is damp and
a small amount of water drains out of the hole.
The seeds you will use may tend to rot if kept too
moist. To avoid inducing the rotting, be sure to
keep the seeds evenly moist, but do not submerge
them. If they do begin to show signs of rotting,
you will need to begin again—a small price to
pay for avoiding contact with chemicals.

6. Observe the pots and plants carefully each day. Remember that young children have a tendency to overwater plants, so be sure to keep the soil evenly damp and see that excess water drains out of the pot.

You should begin to see shoots from the bean seeds emerge from the soil in about two weeks. With a reasonable amount of light your bean plant should continue to grow rapidly, and in about four to six weeks you might even be lucky enough to see a flower or two. The flower may eventually become a bean, and if left on the plant until the bean turns brown, you will have new, dried bean seeds to start the cycle again.

Germinating with Paper Towels

Children cannot see the early stages of bean germination when they are planted in soil. When they germinate bean seeds with paper towels

- All parts of the germination process are easily visible—swelling of the seed, sprouting, the development of roots and shoots

- Children can consider the roles of water, light, and soil in plant survival

There are several methods for this process, but we prefer to place the paper towels in a clear plastic soda bottle.

Materials

- An empty clear plastic soda bottle (preferably one-liter or larger)

- 4 or 5 bean seeds

- 4 or 5 high-quality paper towels

- Plastic coated paper clips

Instructions

1. Cut the top off of the clear plastic bottle so that the bottle is still at least six inches tall.

2. Fold and roll the paper towels so that they cover the inside of the bottle.

3. Put the bean seeds between the paper towels and the inside of the bottle so that they are evenly spaced around the bottle.

4. Clip the paper towels to the bottle with paper clips. This will help to keep the seeds in place.

5. Water the paper towels so that they are wet. Put enough water in the bottle so that the bottom of the paper towels is always in contact with water, thus ensuring the towels will remain constantly moist. Be careful not to allow the seeds themselves to be under water—they should always remain in contact with the moist paper towels. If placed near heat, near the sun, or even in a room on a cold day, the water in the bottle can evaporate quickly, so you will need to pay frequent careful attention.

In the bottle, you will be able to watch the seeds begin to expand in just a few days. The seeds will start to sprout in about a week, first by sending down a root, then by sending up a shoot that eventually will have leaves. The bean plant may continue to grow as it would in soil; however, it is unlikely to be as healthy as it would be in the soil because it will not get certain nutrients that it needs. Putting a bit of plant fertilizer in the water may help.

You may want to germinate a number of beans on a tray inside wet paper towels so children can look closely at them and handle them. Place two paper towels, one atop the other, on a tray or plate. Fold the towels in half. Place three or four seeds in a row on the towels, then fold the towels over the seeds, and water. Keep the towels moist, and unfold them each day to observe changes in the seeds.

BULBS

Materials

- Narcissus bulbs

- Garlic bulbs

- Shallow bowls for narcissus bulbs

- Small planting pots or cups with holes in the bottom for garlic

- Small stones or pebbles for narcissus bulbs

- Potting soil for garlic

Instructions for forcing narcissus bulbs

1. Place an even layer of pebbles into the shallow container.

2. Put the narcissus bulbs into the container so the bottom of each bulb is below the surface of the pebbles.

3. Fill the container with water so the bottoms of the bulbs are actually touching the water.

4. Pay careful attention to the bulbs each day, making sure the bottoms of the bulbs are wet until roots are visible.

5. After the roots are established, be sure there is ample water so the roots are kept wet. At this point there is no need for the bulb itself to be in water.

Instructions for planting garlic cloves

1. Crack a garlic bulb into individual cloves.

2. Fill each pot or cup with soil.

3. Put each clove into the soil, pointy side up, just so the top of the clove is still above the soil line.

4. Water the soil. Keep the soil evenly moist. You should see the green shoot emerge in one to two weeks.

BEET OR CARROT TOPS

Materials

- A beet or carrot with leaves still attached
- Shallow container with water or a pot with soil

Instructions

1. Cut the carrot or beet leaves back almost to the top of the carrot or beet itself, being careful to leave at least a little of the stem growth.

2. Cut off the top 2 inches or more of a carrot or beet.

3. Place the carrot or beet top into a shallow container of water. Do not submerge the entire top.

4. Be sure to keep water in the container so that the cut end of the carrot or beet is always wet (if it becomes dry for too long, the plant will not grow).

5. Watch for growth of the stem out of the top—you should notice growth within a week.

CUTTINGS

Materials

- A begonia, geranium, or other common houseplant
- A container of water

Instructions

1. Cut a stem from a healthy begonia or geranium.

2. Place the cut end in the water. (Be sure to replenish water as needed.)

3. In about two weeks, you should begin to notice small roots growing from the stem. Once the roots are established, you can place the cutting in a pot with soil.

POTATO PLANTS AND OTHER TUBERS

Materials

- Potato
- Pot with soil

Instructions

1. Cut the potato into several pieces, being sure to have at least one eye (dark spot that sometimes sprouts) on each piece.

2. Place each piece of potato in the soil. Cover it completely, keeping it just beneath the soil surface.

3. Keep the soil moist.

For other suggestions for starting plants, refer to *Grow Lab: Activities for Growing Minds*, described on p. 136.

WHERE TO PURCHASE MATERIALS

- Most pet stores sell very small plastic terraria and gravel.
- Pet stores and garden centers sell garden charcoal.
- Hand trowels are available at garden centers or hardware stores.
- Bean seeds are available as dried beans in most local supermarkets.
- For supplies for terraria (containers and gravel), hand lenses, plants, and animals, see the following:

DELTA EDUCATION
P. O. Box 3000
Nashua, NH 03061-3000
800-442-5444
www.delta-education.com

CONNECTICUT VALLEY BIOLOGICAL SUPPLY
82 Valley Road, P. O. Box 326
Southampton, MA 01073
800-628-7748
www.ctvalleybio.com

Insect Lore Products
P. O. Box 1535
Shafter, CA 93263
800-LIVE BUG
www.insectlore.com

The Web site contains information about materials useful for exploring insects with children. You can purchase live insects as well as related books and software.

National Gardening Association
180 Flynn Avenue
Burlington, VT 05401
800-538-7476
www.kidsgardening.com

This Web site contains information about a range of materials related to children and gardening. You can purchase seeds, kits, tools, and other useful materials.

Carolina Biological Supply Company
2700 York Road
Burlington, NC 27215
800-227-1150
www.carolina.com

You can purchase all kinds of live plants and animals here.

Involving Families

A number of children's family members are likely to have knowledge or abilities that will be valuable as you engage in discovering nature. Some will be avid gardeners or will have experience with houseplants. Others will enjoy nature as hikers or bird watchers. Find out which resources exist in your community of families, and try to make use of some family members. These visits enhance both children's learning and the home-to-school connection.

It will be helpful to set the stage for family support early. At the beginning of the exploration, send home the letter to families (p. 131) with each child to introduce families to the exploration. Let them know what children will do and learn, and suggest ways that they can support their children's science learning.

You can also extend children's science learning by suggesting science-related activities for families to do at home and in the community. These activities can reinforce the science children are learning in the classroom and outdoors, while helping children and families

see science phenomena in their daily lives. As the exploration progresses, send home "Families Discovering Nature" (p. 132), which offers nature activities that caregivers can do with their children.

Books and Videos

It is important to evaluate books, videos, and other resources on living things that you select for children to use in the classroom. Select carefully, because the materials that you choose will be valuable resources for the children's explorations. It is important that all resources meet these basic criteria:

- Characters and content should reflect cultural diversity. Not every book and video must represent different cultures, but your collection should as a whole.

- Stereotypes should be absent.

- Content should be scientifically accurate.

The resources for children are listed in two categories—books and videos. The books category is broken into additional subdivisions. Each category contains selection criteria and a set of annotated examples to help you identify high-quality resources. But keep in mind that books go out of print and are not always available. If the examples listed below are not obtainable, use the given criteria to choose others like them. It is best to have different kinds of books and resources available for children to use, and remember that types of books can overlap. For example, a field guide or image book might also be considered an information book.

Finally, there is also a list of resource books and Web sites for teachers that you may find helpful in gathering information about living things and ideas to use in the classroom. Specific Web sites may change; those listed are examples of the kinds of sites that can support the exploration.

Books for Children

Nonfiction

Listed below are four different kinds of nonfiction books for children: field guides, image books, information books, and biographies. Each of these nonfiction books has at least three criteria in common—scientifically accurate content; detailed illustrations or photo-

SAMPLE LETTER TO FAMILIES

Dear Families,

You may have noticed that your children are naturally curious about the world around them. They may be especially excited and interested in the animal and plant life they encounter in their everyday lives—chasing butterflies, watching ants crawl on the ground, and noticing plants growing and flowers budding in the springtime.

As part of our science curriculum this year we are going to study living things. Your children will develop a scientific approach to their investigation of the outdoors as they become naturalists studying the local environment, looking for living things, and discovering how and where they live. The children will also gain an appreciation and respect for the environment. We will teach your children to observe and study living things without disrupting or disturbing them.

At school, your children will do the following:

- Observe living things closely, outdoors and indoors
- Make observational drawings to show what they have seen in their observations
- Create temporary habitats for plants and animals they find outdoors
- Research in books to learn more about the things they find
- Share their thinking and ideas about what living things they found, what they look like, how they move, and what they need

You can really help our explorations by maintaining a positive and upbeat attitude toward all living creatures. As adults, we have all exclaimed at one point or another, "Don't touch that!" or "Yuck, that's disgusting!" as our children enthusiastically present us with a grub or worm while exploring and discovering the outdoors. Your children will be delighted if, instead, you encourage their explorations and show an interest in their discoveries, and even share your own observations—a butterfly your child missed or your favorite kind of flower growing in a garden.

We can also use your assistance and expertise at school. If you have time to volunteer, come help us as we explore. An extra pair of hands is always welcome. Or if you are knowledgeable about plants, bugs, flowers, insects, gardening, or anything else related to our study, let us know. We'd love to have you share your experience with all the children.

Finally, please let us know if your child has any allergies that we should be aware of, such as to bees, pollen, grass, and so on, so your child can fully enjoy looking at the world through a scientist's eyes!

---

graphs that give children information and stimulate ideas; and content that is inherently interesting to children, stimulates their exploration, and raises questions for them.

Field Guides

These are books that will help children identify the plants and animals they are discovering and exploring. Photographs and illustrations should be detailed and in color so children can see the differences between types of plants or types of animals. Field guides also provide basic information about habitat, needs, and some behaviors.

Examples of field guides include the following:

- Eyewitness Explorers. Titles include *Butterflies and Moths, Flowers, Trees,* and *Insects.* New York: DK Publishing.

- National Audubon Society First Guides. Titles include *Birds, Insects, Trees,* and *Wildflowers.* New York: Scholastic.

- Peterson First Guides. Titles include *Butterflies and Moths, Caterpillars, Insects, Trees,* and *Wildflowers.* Boston: Houghton Mifflin.

- Peterson First Guides for Young Naturalists. Titles include *Butterflies* and *Caterpillars.* Boston: Houghton Mifflin.

FAMILIES DISCOVERING NATURE

Whether you are a gardener or have had no experience growing plants, or whether you are a pet lover or feel uncomfortable around bugs or other animals, you can become a naturalist with your child. What's most important is to try to maintain a positive attitude and resist any temptation to squash a bug or show your fear, as your child will certainly follow your lead. Your child will be delighted if, instead, you encourage her explorations. And by exploring plants and animals together, you and your child will learn more about each other and the natural world around you.

Tips for Outdoor Explorations

Take a naturalist walk with your child in a park, your neighborhood, or backyard. Bring along clipboards, paper, and pencils so that as you and your child observe, both of you can sketch the plants and animals you see, trying to capture the details. Bring a field guide of your local area and a hand lens if you have them.

During your naturalist walk, you and your child can note the following:

- Plants and animals you see
- Characteristics of each plant or animal (such as its shape, color, size, and texture)
- Different parts of each plant or animal (such as leaves, branches, stems, and trunk, or eyes, legs, and antennae)
- Movements made by animals (such as squirming, flying, crawling, or creeping)
- Place where you found the plants and animals (such as on the ground, on a wall, under a log or rock, or in the air)
- Ways the different plants are alike and different
- Ways the different animals are alike and different

In addition to exploring the plants and animals in your neighborhood, you might also plan trips to greenhouses, plant nurseries, woods, pond areas, and so on. By exploring different areas, you and your child can compare and contrast the kinds of plants animals found in new environments to those living in and around your neighborhood.

Tips for Indoor Explorations

You might also want to grow different types of houseplants, so your child can see how different types of plants grow and change over time. At the same time, you can notice together how different plants are alike and different. Or, if you're feeling adventurous, you and your child can build a terrarium for some short-term animal visitors. You will need the following:

- Large, clear container with fine-mesh (small holes) cover
- Large rubber bands or tape (to secure the cover)
- Gravel, pebbles, or sand (for drainage)
- A hand trowel or small shovel
- A water bottle for keeping the soil moist

With your child, put about one inch of the pebbles or sand at the bottom of the container. Put several inches of dirt on top of the pebbles or sand. Also put in a few small plants, such as grass, moss, tree seedlings, and weeds. Moisten the soil by adding water; mist the leaves of plants. Cover the container, then place it inside out of direct sunlight. Then with your child, collect small animals such as worms, pillbugs, grubs, and snails; put them in the terrarium. Spend a week observing, drawing, and talking about the plants and animals you see. Then return the animals to the environment where you found them.

Tips for Naturalist Talks

As your child explores different plants and animals, use these tips to spark some conversations:

- Invite your child to tell you about the plant or animal she saw and where she found it. ("Tell me about the plant you found.")
- Help your child think about the characteristics of the plant or animal. ("What does the plant or animal look like? What color is it? How big is it? What shape is it? How does it feel when you touch it?")
- Help your child think about an animal's behavior and needs. ("How does the worm move? How do you think it can get underground? What do you think it needs to live? Why?")
- Wonder out loud with your child. ("I wonder what would happen if we put the worm on the table. Would it crawl off? . . . I wonder what will happen to the plant when it gets really, really cold outside.")

Provide your child with the support he needs to share his thinking:

- Give your child time to think before he responds to your questions and comments. Silent time is okay.
- Find ways for your child to show you what he knows (for example, using his hands to show you how an animal moves).

Avoid comments that could limit your child's thinking. Avoid the following:

- Explaining the science
- Correcting ideas (rather, ask more questions)
- Moving on too quickly (allow the child to decide when to move on)

Image Books

Image books for children ages three through five are any books that use large, detailed illustrations or photographs to convey information and inspire children to explore further. These can include books that are specifically written for children or books that are meant for adults or older children but have engaging pictures that inform and stimulate young children's thinking.

Examples of image books include the following:

- Greenaway, Theresa. 2000. *Big Book of Bugs*. New York: DK Publishing.

  Stunning, larger-than-life photographs provide children with detailed information about many different kinds of bugs. Accompanying text presents many facts.

- Oppenheim, Joanne. 1996. *Have You Seen Bugs?* New York: Scholastic Press.

  Rhyming verse describes many different bugs and how they eat, move, and work. Beautiful images that are actually paper sculptures bring the world of bugs to life.

- Stefoff, Rebecca. 1998. *Ant*. Tarrytown, N.Y.: Benchmark Books.

  Large, clear photographs show ants up close in their natural habitats. Accompanying text provides interesting facts about ants, such as what they eat and how they live, and describes different kinds of ants, including carpenter ants and army ants. Other titles in this Living Things series include *Beetle*, *Butterfly*, *Frog*, and *Praying Mantis*.

Information Books

Information books for children ages three through five are books that focus on specific topics, such as ants, frogs, beans, the desert, or plants. Or they can be books that focus on specific questions such as "How do plants grow?" or "Where do ants live?" These books provide children with information that answers questions and raises more questions.

Examples of information books include the following:

- Burnie, David. 2000. *Plant*. Eyewitness Book Series. New York: DK Publishing.

  Beautiful real-life photographs of flowers, fruits, seeds, leaves, and more deliver a unique "eyewitness" view. Provides a wealth of information about how a dandelion spreads its seeds, how plants defend themselves, why flowers are brightly colored, and much more. Other titles in the series include *Butterfly and Moth*, *Pond and River*, *Reptile*, *Shell*, and *Tree*.

- Johnson, Sylvia A. 1982. *Snails*. Lerner Natural Science Book. Minneapolis: Lerner Publications.

  With excellent photographs and vivid descriptions, this book provides an introduction to land snails and also looks at some snails that live in watery environments. There are many great titles in this series including *Ants*, *Beetles*, *Chirping Insects*, *Fireflies*, *How Leaves Change*, *How Seeds Travel*, *Mosses*, and *Wasps*.

- Julivert, Angels. 1991. *The Fascinating World of . . . Butterflies and Moths*. Hauppauge, N.Y.: Barrons Educational Series, Inc.

  This series of books offers full-color illustrations of a variety of living creatures. Each creature is shown in detail, and body parts are labeled and described. Although the accompanying text is for older children, the extensive information given is valuable for young children as well. Other titles in the series include *Ants*, *Bees*, *Spiders*, and *Frogs and Toads*.

Biographies

Biographies for children ages three through five are real stories about real people. Biographical characters should be related to the topic of study, and the story should be focused and comprehensible enough for children this age.

Examples of biographies include the following:

- Brandenberg, Aliki. 1987. *The Story of Johnny Appleseed*. New York: Aladdin Paperbacks.

  This book tells the story of John Chapman, a celebrated figure in history who was dedicated to planting apple trees all across the country.

- Brandenberg, Aliki. 1988. *A Weed Is a Flower: The Life of George Washington Carver*. New York: Aladdin Paperbacks.

  This book tells the story of George Washington Carver, who was well known for his successes in agricultural research and his development of hundreds of uses for peanuts and other plants.

FICTION

Listed below are two different kinds of fiction books for children: fact and fantasy and real-life fiction. Each of these fiction books has at least three of the following criteria in common—developmentally appropriate presentation (rhythm, repetition, story length, vocabulary, font size); content that is inherently interesting to children, stimulates their exploration, and raises questions for them; illustrations that explain the story; and a substantial amount of scientifically accurate content.

Fact and Fantasy

A major feature of fact and fantasy books for children ages three through five is that they should raise questions for children about scientific phenomena and spark their interests. Books that view the natural world through the eyes of different cultures can help children begin to understand science from different perspectives. While much of the content should be scientifically accurate, these books may also contain some fantasy.

Examples of fact and fantasy books for children include the following:

- Caduto, Michael, and Joseph Bruchac. 1997. *Keepers of Life: Discovering Plants through Native American Stories and Earth Activities for Children.* Golden, Colo.: Fulcrum Publishing.

  This collection of nineteen Native American stories and activities exposes children to the concept of interdependence, that all living things are connected. The book is a beautiful assortment of tales that will stimulate children's curiosity and interest in plants and nature.

- Doolittle, Bev, and Elise Maclay. 1998. *The Forest Has Eyes.* Shelton, Conn.: The Greenwich Workshop Press.

  Children will need to use their observation skills to look at this collection of paintings of Native Americans and the wilderness. Each painting has images hidden behind and within other images, and the text describes different features of Native American culture and history. Together they will inspire children to think about living things in the natural world.

- Lionni, Leo. 1987. *The Biggest House in the World.* New York: Pantheon Books.

  Colorful illustrations enrich the simple text that tells the story of a snail who wishes for a bigger house. His wish comes true but he eventually realizes that his new big house doesn't suit him. Children will enjoy the fantasy in this story while also thinking about why the snail's initial shell was the best one for him.

- Mazer, Anne. 1991. *The Salamander Room.* New York: Alfred A. Knopf.

  This is a story about a boy who finds a salamander in the woods and imagines how to make his home a perfect home for the salamander. While it does contain some fantasy, it is ideal for getting children to think about the needs of living things that come to visit in the classroom.

Real-Life Fiction

These books differ from other fiction books because, while the story is fictional, the science content is accurate. Where other fiction books might contain bits of fantasy, these do not. Similar to fact and fantasy books, real-life fiction books should also raise questions for children about scientific phenomena.

Examples of real-life fiction books for children include the following:

- Chrustowski, Rick. 2000. *Bright Beetle.* New York: Henry Holt and Company.

  This book follows one of a ladybug's eggs from larva to adulthood as she encounters and defends herself against ants and a praying mantis. The detailed, accurate story introduces children to the concept of a life cycle.

- Fleming, Denise. 1991. *In the Tall, Tall Grass.* New York: Henry Holt and Company.

  This book takes children on a tour of a backyard and what they might find in the tall grass. Basic rhyming text and colorful illustrations will encourage children to take a closer look at what is in their own environment.

- Pattou, Edith. 2001. *Mrs. Spitzer's Garden.* New York: Harcourt, Inc.

  The underlying theme of this book is how children will thrive if tended carefully like a garden. It also provides a real picture of the factors involved in growing plants and flowers, as well as introducing concepts of variation, diversity, and the different needs of different living things.

POETRY

Poetry for children ages three through five encompasses characteristics of both fiction and nonfiction books. It can be either completely scientifically accurate or contain bits of fantasy and should contain content that is inherently interesting to children, stimulates their exploration, and raises questions for them. Unlike other books for children, however, poetry uses words rather than pictures to illustrate experiences and phenomena, often containing rhyming verses. This does not mean that these books will have no pictures, just that the words will be able to draw a picture themselves.

Examples of poetry books include the following:

- Florian, Douglas. 1998. *Insectlopedia*. New York: Harcourt Brace & Company.

  This collection of poems will keep children engaged with its beautiful watercolor paintings and whimsical rhyming verse and word play. It blends science with fantasy, as in "The Inchworm": "I inch, I arch, I march along. I'm just a pinch, a mere inch long. I stroll and stick on sticks in thickets, and never pick up speeding tickets."

- Florian, Douglas. 2001. *Lizards, Frogs, and Polliwogs.* New York: Harcourt Brace & Company.

  Another collection of poems by Florian, these are about reptiles and amphibians.

VIDEOS FOR CHILDREN

Is it valuable or appropriate for children ages three through five to spend much time watching videos? When contemplating the use of videos in your classroom, the most important thing to consider is whether the video is actually being used in ways that enrich children's experiences, or *in place of* the experiences? If not the former, it may well be worth passing up. Other criteria include developmentally appropriate content; scientifically accurate content; and content that is inherently interesting to children, stimulates their exploration, and raises questions for them.

Videos for young children can provide a great deal of information, presenting it more actively than books. A video can show the details of a worm moving or fast-forward through the life cycle of a plant or animal in a short period of time, something that a book cannot do.

Examples of videos include the following:

- Eyewitness Videos. New York: DK Publishing. The Eyewitness Videos series are thirty-minute videos that present information on a range of topics using nature photography, graphics, facts, and folk stories. They will keep children engaged and prompt them to ask many questions. Titles include *Reptile, Insect, Plant, Bird,* and *Amphibian.*

- Tell Me Why. Venice, Calif.: TMW Media Group. Each video in this series is thirty minutes long and answers questions children may have on a variety of topics. Each video also comes with a study guide that contains a glossary and further questions. Titles include *Flowers, Plants and Trees,* and *Insects.* These videos are also available in Spanish.

RESOURCE BOOKS AND WEB SITES FOR TEACHERS

These resources should be used only by the teacher to gather information, get ideas to use in the classroom, or find tips on caring for plants and animals. The main criterion for these resources is that they should contain scientifically accurate content. Although the books will not be used by young children, it may be helpful if they are written simply and clearly so teachers can access information without wading through difficult scientific language. Also be aware that any Web sites listed here might be discontinued. They are listed as examples of the kinds of information available on the Web.

RESOURCE BOOKS

- Hartley, Karen, and Chris Macro. 1998. *Snail.* Des Plaines, Ill.: Heinemann Library.

  This book, one in the Bug Books series, is filled with fascinating close-up photos of snails and answers to many snail questions. This also fits into the information books category.

- Lawrence Hall of Science. 1997. *Terrarium Habitats.* Berkeley, Calif.: Lawrence Hall of Science.

  This teachers' guide from Great Explorations in Math and Science (GEMS) is one of a series from the Lawrence Hall of Science at the University of California, Berkeley. Check out the GEMS Web site at www.lhs.berkeley.edu/GEMS.

- National Gardening Association. 1990. *GrowLab: Activities for Growing Minds.* Burlington, Vt.: National Gardening Association.

This resource book has many activities to use with children in the classroom and provides essential "how-to" information for teachers about planting.

- Parker, Steve. 1992. *The Random House Book of How Nature Works.* New York: Random House.

  Supplies background information on how animals meet their needs and how they grow, move, and protect themselves. Includes detailed illustrations.

- Russell, Helen Ross. 1997. *Ten-Minute Field Trips: Using the School Grounds for Environmental Studies.* 3d ed. Washington, D.C.: National Science Teachers Association.

  This book includes more than 200 field trip ideas for urban, suburban, and rural settings where children can explore their local environments in new ways.

- Simon, Seymour. 1988. *Pets in a Jar: Collecting and Caring for Small Wild Animals.* New York: Penguin.

  Provides many tips on how to select a pet, which containers work best to keep them, what they need to survive, and where and how to release them.

WEB SITES

- *www.msue.msu.edu*

  Michigan State University Extension Web site contains detailed information about constructing and maintaining a terrarium, including a list of plants that are appropriate to grow in one.

- *www.kiddyhouse.com*

  Kiddyhouse.com presents basic information about land and pond snails that is pertinent to teachers who are inviting these animals into their classrooms.

- *www.kidsource.com*

  KidSource OnLine contains an article about recognizing poison ivy and its cousins.

- *www.kidsgardening.com*

  This National Gardening Association site has a host of information on composting, including stories of classrooms that have used compost. The site also contains an FAQ called "Gardening Safely with Kids."

- *www.poisonivy.aesir.com*

  This is the site of the Poison Ivy, Oak, and Sumac Information Center.

- *www.techandyoungchildren.org*

  The Technology and Young Children Web site provides many links to articles on using computers and other technology with young children.

- *www.blackjungle.com*

  Black Jungle Terrarium Supply specializes in making and maintaining terraria. They provide suggestions for plants and animals, as well as the materials for meeting their needs.

- *www.botit.botany.wisc.edu*

  The University of Wisconsin, Madison's Department of Botany Web site offers wonderful photographs of bean plants at different stages of development.

- *www.yahooligans.com*

  Yahooligans is a search engine designed specifically for children that may help teachers find Web sites with clear, plainly worded information on living things. Most of the sites that come up in a search, however, are not appropriate for children ages three through five to use.

appendices

Suggestions for Long-Term Representation Projects

PLANTS

Observational drawing is an essential feature of *Discovering Nature with Young Children*. One way to focus children's observations and thinking about growth and development is to help them compile a journal of drawings. Other ways you can help children begin and maintain a record of what they notice about a plant, its parts, and how the parts work together to help it meet its needs include the following:

- Offer children sculpting materials like craft wire, clay, and plasticine so they can create representations of their plant's stems, trunks, and branches. If your children aren't familiar with these materials, allow them to explore and create during choice time for a few weeks before you suggest they use the materials to represent plants or animals.

- Ask children to choose a tree, bush, or other plant that they can represent over time. Invite children to choose a sculpting material that they'd like to use to make their plant's structure.

- Provide the children with a base on which to stand their sculpture. Two-inch-thick pieces of Styrofoam work well for holding up wire. Pieces of wood work well as bases for clay and plasticine.

- Write the words children use to describe their plant's stem, trunk, or branch and its texture, color, or thickness, or the way it moves or doesn't move in the wind. Post next to the sculpture.

Help children dramatize their observations:

- Ask children to choose a tree, bush, or other plant that they can observe over time.

- Invite children to shape their bodies as the stem, trunk, and branches on their plant.

- Ask them to pretend it's windy and to move as they think their plant might move in the wind.

- You might want to supply pieces of fabric that children can wrap around themselves or hold to represent their plant's stem or trunk, and their leaves.

Provide interested children with materials to measure and graph their plant's height or number of leaves over time. Create a class book of observational drawings, notes, and photographs documenting the changes in the tree or bush the children observe each month.

ANIMALS

When children begin to study an animal life cycle, use the following suggestions to help children record and reflect on the changes an animal goes through as it moves from one stage of its life cycle to the next.

- Offer children sculpting materials like craft wire, clay, and plasticine so they can create representations of a snail or caterpillar as it goes through different stages of its life cycle. Also, identify a display shelf for these sculptures and models. Label each one with the child's name and invite her to dictate a sentence or two about it to add to the sign.

- Help children dramatize their observations. As children observe an animal go through each part of its life cycle, they can act it out. Provide space, time, and materials for making costumes and props so children can act out what they are learning about their animal's life cycle over and over again. Teachers and children can take turns narrating the dramatization as children perform for each other.

- Create a class book of children's annotated drawings, photographs of their representational models, and photographs of their dramatizations of the animals' life cycles.

- Keep individual caterpillar or snail journals of regular observational drawings. If children are inclined, add their own words to record what they observe.

CLASSROOM ENVIRONMENT CHECKLIST

Classroom Materials Inventory

Complete an inventory of the materials you have for the "Discovering Nature" exploration by filling in the middle column of the chart below. In the right column, list what you need to obtain. Refer to pp. 16–18 of the teacher's guide for a more complete list of recommended materials.

Item	Inventory	Needs
Hand lens		
Bug boxes		
Penlights		
Containers for collecting		
Large terrarium		
Gravel, charcoal		
Flower pots or plastic containers		
Potting soil, bean seeds		
Plant sprayer		
Clipboards, pencils, paper		
Hand trowels		
Tongue depressors		
Plexiglass		
Measuring tape		
Field guide and other books		

Set Up the Classroom

Complete the chart below to help you plan how your space will reflect your study of living things. Use the check column on the right to note your accomplishments. See p. 18 in the teacher's guide for specific recommendations.

Recommendations	Plans	✔
Surface for terrarium		
Wall space		
Book space		
Table space for three-dimensional work		
Accessible materials and tool storage		

Plan the Schedule

Two special times for naturalist work are recommended on p. 19 of the teacher's guide: outdoor time and planning and reflection time. Use the following chart to assess your needs and plan necessary changes to your daily schedule.

Time	Current Schedule	Change in Schedule
Outdoor time At least 30 minutes twice per week for outdoor exploration		
Choice time 30–45 minutes of choice time at least three times per week		
Science talk 10–15 minutes as a whole group at least once per week		

Find Outdoor Space for Exploration

You will need at least one space to explore outdoors with your children. Consider your playground, other places on the premises, and nearby parks or fields. Look for the following:

- A variety of plants such as flowers, weeds, bushes, and trees
- Small animals such as snails, ants, pill bugs, and/or worms
- Larger animals such as birds and squirrels
- Accessibility to classroom
- Activities for children who are not exploring
- Safety from glass, poisonous plants, and traffic

Identify what you have found on this chart.

Specific Location	What You Found

GUIDELINES FOR CREATING DOCUMENTATION PANELS

How Do I Make a Documentation Panel?

1. Collect documents.

- Collect related work samples—drawings, paintings, and photos of children's three-dimensional representations.

- Collect dialogue. Record science-related conversations with and among children, jot down a conversation that can be typed up later, or ask children to tell you about their work or a photo.

- Pull together notes and data that have been collected during the exploration—science inquiry charts, a list of predictions, descriptive observations, new questions, and so on.

- If you have access to a camera, take photos of children making science-related observations or interacting with living things. Get close-ups of children's hands and faces. Enlarge 3- by 5-inch and 4- by 6-inch photos on a photocopier, or print digital photos on 8- by 11-inch paper (the photos should be large enough for a group of children to view together).

2. Decide the panel's focus.

- Discovery—Children discover pill bugs under rotting logs, bricks, stones, and old leaves.

- Exploration—Children explore a local park for living things. Where do they look? What do they see?

- Data collection—Children measure the breadth of various maple trees, or they sequence a dozen oak leaves by size, from smallest to largest.

- Comparison—Children compare and contrast the snails and slugs in their classroom terrarium to the ones they saw during their visit to a greenhouse.

- Tool use—Children use hand lenses, penlights, and bug boxes to look more closely.

How Do I Put Together the Panel?

1. Arrange your documents in chronological order, from left to right, across the board in a single, straight line. Adhere your photos with a glue stick, rubber cement, or two-sided tape. (White glue wrinkles paper.)

2. Add text to your panel. Suggestions include the following:

- Interview the children whose work is featured on the panel and use some of their words as captions under their work samples.

- Add the question or challenge that guided the children's focused exploration.

- Add the names of the tools children were using.

3. Add a title that focuses your reading audience on the panel's key message. For example:

- Max uses a hand lens to look very closely.

- Making a terrarium for our snails.

How Can I Display the Panels and Share Them with Families?

- Post the panels at children's eye level. When you run out of wall space, move the ones that aren't currently being using into the hall or to some other location where families and colleagues might enjoy them.

- Invite children to share panels with family members. Post a couple of questions next to the panel to prompt conversation and help focus it on the aspect of science inquiry featured on the panel.

- Share panels during parent conferences. Use them to reflect on specific aspects of children's science experiences and their growth and development.

OBSERVATION RECORD

Teacher_____ Date: _____

Setting:_____

Check one: ☐ Open Exploration   ☐ Focused Exploration

Check one: ☐ Plants   ☐ Animals

Step: _____

Children's Names	Seen and Heard

DOCUMENT ANNOTATION

Child(ren): _____ Date: _____

Context/Setting: _____

_____

_____

Science Concepts Explored/Evidence: _____

_____

_____

DOCUMENT ANNOTATION

Child(ren): _____ Date: _____

Context/Setting: _____

_____

_____

Science Concepts Explored/Evidence: _____

_____

_____

DOCUMENT ANNOTATION

Child(ren): _____ Date: _____

Context/Setting: _____

_____

_____

Science Concepts Explored/Evidence: _____

_____

_____

LEARNING RECORD: PART I

Child _____ Birth Date: _____

Date Exploration Begun: _____ Completed: _____

Science Inquiry Skills	Child Growth	Evidence
Engages, notices, wonders, questions	☐ Emerging ☐ Sometimes ☐ Consistently	
Begins to explore, investigate	☐ Emerging ☐ Sometimes ☐ Consistently	
Collects data	☐ Emerging ☐ Sometimes ☐ Consistently	
Records and represents experience	☐ Emerging ☐ Sometimes ☐ Consistently	
Reflects on experience	☐ Emerging ☐ Sometimes ☐ Consistently	
Uses language to communicate feelings	☐ Emerging ☐ Sometimes ☐ Consistently	
Shares, discusses, and reflects with group	☐ Emerging ☐ Sometimes ☐ Consistently	

LEARNING RECORD: PART II

Child _____   **Birth Date:** _____

Date Exploration Begun: _____   **Completed:** _____

Science Concepts	Child Growth	Evidence
Characteristics of living things	☐ Emerging ☐ Sometimes ☐ Consistently	
Living and nonliving	☐ Emerging ☐ Sometimes ☐ Consistently	
Needs of living things	☐ Emerging ☐ Sometimes ☐ Consistently	
Life cycle	☐ Emerging ☐ Sometimes ☐ Consistently	
Diversity and variation	☐ Emerging ☐ Sometimes ☐ Consistently	
Habitat	☐ Emerging ☐ Sometimes ☐ Consistently	

Outcomes Charts

The two outcomes charts that follow will help you to describe and record your children's progress. You may also find them useful when talking with others about the goals of *Discovering Nature with Young Children*. The first chart, "Science Outcomes," is in two parts: science inquiry skills and science concepts. Each skill or concept is defined in the column on the left. On the right are three levels of behaviors, starting with simple and moving to more complex. What your children will achieve will depend on their level of maturity and prior experiences.

The second chart is "Connections between Inquiry Skills and Outcomes in Other Domains." This chart provides a visual presentation of how science inquiry skills relate to outcomes or skills in other areas. The inquiry skills are listed in the left-hand column. Language, literacy, and mathematics skills, as well as social abilities and approach to learning, appear at the top. Checked boxes show where inquiry skills support abilities in other areas. While the outcomes of other subject areas listed are based on the Head Start Child Outcomes Framework, they are also relevant to a range of early childhood programs.

Science Outcomes: Science Inquiry Skills and Science Concepts

Science Inquiry Skills	Naturalist Behaviors
Engages, notices, wonders, questions: Engages in open-ended explorations of living things in different environments; forms questions that guide actions.	• Searches for and finds different plants and small animals in the natural environment. • Observes various plants and animals, noticing similarities and differences in appearance and behavior; wonders why. • Focuses observations on particular characteristics or behaviors; poses questions.
Begins to explore, investigate: Engages in simple investigations to extend observations, test predictions, and pursue questions.	• Asks "what if" ("What if I put the worm over here?"); revisits a plant or animal to observe more closely. • Focuses on a specific question that can be answered. ("How does the snail move?") • Participates in designing simple investigations. ("Let's put lettuce and cabbage in the terrarium and see which one the snail likes.")
Collects data: Uses senses, varied tools, and simple measures to gather data.	• Uses sight and touch when gathering information about living things. • Uses hand lens and penlights to better see details of plants and animals; uses hearing and smell. • Uses string, rulers, and other tools to get quantitative data on living things (such as length, area, weight, and diameter).
Records and represents experience: Describes and records experiences and information through a variety of means, including two- and three-dimensional representation, charts, and movement.	• Demonstrates observations through body movements; makes simple drawings that may incorporate one characteristic of a plant or animal. • Creates two- and three-dimensional representations that incorporate several characteristics of a plant or animal. • Participates in creating a chart that records comparative data from an investigation; makes detailed, realistic drawings.
Reflects on experiences: Explores patterns and relationships among experiences; makes reasonable predictions, explanations, and generalizations based on experience.	• Draws on prior experiences when describing, comparing, and talking about experiences. • Bases predictions and explanations on observations and data from past experiences. • Connects observations and data from multiple explorations, identifying patterns and relationships and stating conclusions.
Uses language to communicate findings: Develops increased vocabulary and ability to communicate observations and ideas.	• Responds to direct questions about physical characteristics of living things and recent experiences. • Contributes more detailed descriptions and ideas about living things to discussions. ("Look—the tail is so long!") • Mentions various characteristics (such as shape, color, size, or names of body parts) when describing a plant or animal; shares questions, ideas, and speculations.

SCIENCE OUTCOMES: SCIENCE INQUIRY SKILLS AND SCIENCE CONCEPTS (CONT'D)

Science Inquiry Skills	Naturalist Behaviors
Shares, discusses, and reflects with group: Shares materials, tasks, and ideas; collaborates in joint investigations.	• Works alone or alongside others (such as sharing a trowel to dig worms for the classroom). • Takes part with a small group of children (such as studying a tree). • In a small group, plans, conducts, and reports on a simple experiment (such as examining what mealworms eat).

Science Concepts	Naturalist Behaviors
Characteristics of living things: Shows a growing awareness of physical characteristics of plants and animals (such as parts, shapes, colors, textures, or sizes); and describes basic behavioral characteristics.	• Identifies basic characteristics of plant and/or animal (such as color, size, and shape). • Identifies more detailed physical characteristics and simple behaviors (such as movement or eating). • Begins to think about simple functions of different parts and relationship to structure. ("The snail has gooey stuff that helps it move.")
Living and nonliving: Shows a growing ability to classify living and nonliving things.	• Uses one or two criteria, such as motion or eating, to define living and nonliving. • Starts to identify categories of things that are not living but move, such as machines or cars; talks about some plants as living things. • Can differentiate living and nonliving things and recognizes that living things do not always move.
Needs of living things: Develops an understanding that living things have basic needs including (for most) water, food, light, air, and space.	• Is aware that living things have needs; tends to attribute own needs to other animals, such as a place to play or toilet. • Begins to understand that all animals need food, water, and a place to live and that plants need water. • Understands that plants and animals have certain basic needs, but they're met in different ways.
Life cycle: Shows an increasing awareness that all living things go through a life cycle, consisting of birth or germination, growth and development, reproduction, and death.	• Talks about baby plants and animals, mommies and daddies, and growing bigger with reference to self. • Describes parts of the life cycle of plants and animals in the classroom or outdoors (such as observing that a caterpillar changes to a butterfly but is uncertain it is the same organism). • Describes the life cycle of a particular plant and/or animal; begins to include reproduction and death; and sees changes connected with the same organism.
Diversity and variation: Develops an awareness of the diversity of living things and variation within species.	• Notices that there are different plants and animals; makes very basic comparisons (such as big/little; bug/"animal"). • Can compare observable similarities and differences among living things (such as leaves of most plants are green; snails have eyes like we do). • Can categorize plants and animals and describe variation within categories (such as leaves from different plants have different shapes; monarch butterflies have similar colors but different patterns from painted lady butterflies).
Habitat: Develops growing awareness and understanding that plants and animals have their needs met in particular ways in particular places.	• Returns to similar environments looking for a particular plant or animal. • Contributes ideas to discussions about what specific animals or plants want or need. ("The worm likes dirt.") • Helps to plan the development of an indoor environment for a particular organism; has specific ideas related to that organism.

CONNECTIONS BETWEEN INQUIRY SKILLS AND OUTCOMES IN OTHER DOMAINS

LANGUAGE and **SCIENCE**	Shows progress in understanding and following simple and multistep directions.	Shows increasing abilities to understand and use language to communicate information, experience, ideas, feelings, opinions, questions, and so on.	Progresses in abilities to initiate and respond appropriately in conversation and discussions with peers and adults.	Links new learning experiences and vocabulary to what is already known about a topic.
Explores/questions—Engages in open-ended explorations; forms questions that guide actions.		✓	✓	
Begins to investigate—Engages in simple investigations to extend observations, test predictions, and pursue questions.	✓	✓	✓	✓
Collects data—Uses senses, varied tools, and simple measures to gather data.	✓	✓		
Records and represents experience—Describes and records experiences and information through a variety of means, including two- and three-dimensional representation, charts, and movement.		✓		✓
Synthesizes and analyzes data from experiences—Sees patterns in data and relationships among experiences; makes reasonable predictions, explanations, and generalizations based on experience.		✓	✓	✓
Uses language to communicate findings—Develops increased vocabulary and ability to communicate observations and ideas.		✓	✓	✓
Collaborates—Shares materials, tasks, and ideas; collaborates in joint investigations.		✓	✓	

CONNECTIONS BETWEEN INQUIRY SKILLS AND OUTCOMES IN OTHER DOMAINS (CONT'D)

LITERACY and SCIENCE	Progresses in abilities to retell and dictate stories from books or experiences, act out stories in dramatic play, and predict what will happen next in a story.	Develops an understanding that writing is a way of communicating for a variety of purposes.	Begins to represent stories and experiences through pictures, dictation, and play.	Experiments with a growing variety of writing tools, such as pencils, crayons, and computers.
Explores/questions—Engages in open-ended explorations; forms questions that guide actions.				
Begins to investigate—Engages in simple investigations to extend observations, test predictions, and pursue questions.	✓			
Collects data—Uses senses, varied tools, and simple measures to gather data.		✓		✓
Records and represents experience—Describes and records experiences and information through a variety of means, including two- and three-dimensional representation, charts, and movement.	✓	✓	✓	✓
Synthesizes and analyzes data from experiences—Sees patterns in data and relationships among experiences; makes reasonable predictions, explanations, and generalizations based on experience.	✓	✓	✓	✓
Uses language to communicate findings—Develops increased vocabulary and ability to communicate observations and ideas.	✓	✓	✓	✓
Collaborates—Shares materials, tasks, and ideas; collaborates in joint investigations.				

CONNECTIONS BETWEEN INQUIRY SKILLS AND OUTCOMES IN OTHER DOMAINS (CONT'D)

MATHEMATICS and SCIENCE	Begins to recognize, describe, compare, and name common shapes and their parts and attributes.	Increases understanding of directionality, order, positions of objects, and words (up, down, over, under, top, bottom, and so on).	Enhances abilities to recognize, duplicate, and extend simple patterns using a variety of materials.	Increases abilities to match, sort, put in a series, regroup, and compare objects according to one or two attributes (such as shape or size).	Shows progress in using standard and nonstandard measures for length and area of objects.	Participates in creating and using real and pictorial graphs.
Explores/questions—Engages in open-ended explorations; forms questions that guide actions.						
Begins to investigate—Engages in simple investigations to extend observations, test predictions, and pursue questions.				✓	✓	✓
Collects data—Uses senses, varied tools, and simple measures to gather data.	✓	✓		✓	✓	✓
Records and represents experience—Describes and records experiences and information through a variety of means, including two- and three-dimensional representation, charts, and movement.	✓	✓		✓	✓	✓
Synthesizes and analyzes data from experiences—Sees patterns in data and relationships among experiences; makes reasonable predictions, explanations, and generalizations based on experience.	✓	✓	✓	✓		✓
Uses language to communicate findings—Develops increased vocabulary and ability to communicate observations and ideas.	✓	✓				
Collaborates—Shares materials, tasks, and ideas; collaborates in joint investigations.						

CONNECTIONS BETWEEN INQUIRY SKILLS AND OUTCOMES IN OTHER DOMAINS (CONT'D)

SOCIAL and SCIENCE	Demonstrates increasing capacity to follow rules and routines; uses materials purposefully, safely, and respectfully.	Increases abilities to compromise in interactions, take turns, and sustain interactions with peers by helping, sharing, and discussing.	Progresses in understanding similarities and respecting differences among people (such as gender, race, special needs, culture, and so on).	Develops growing awareness of jobs and what is required to perform them.
Explores/questions—Engages in open-ended explorations; forms questions that guide actions.	✓	✓	✓	✓
Begins to investigate—Engages in simple investigations to extend observations, test predictions, and pursue questions.	✓	✓	✓	✓
Collects data—Uses senses, varied tools, and simple measures to gather data.	✓	✓	✓	✓
Records and represents experience—Describes and records experiences and information through a variety of means, including two- and three-dimensional representation, charts, and movement.	✓	✓	✓	✓
Synthesizes and analyzes data from experiences—Sees patterns in data and relationships among experiences; makes reasonable predictions, explanations, and generalizations based on experience.	✓	✓	✓	✓
Uses language to communicate findings—Develops increased vocabulary and ability to communicate observations and ideas.	✓	✓	✓	✓
Collaborates—Shares materials, tasks, and ideas; collaborates in joint investigations.	✓	✓	✓	✓

CONNECTIONS BETWEEN INQUIRY SKILLS AND OUTCOMES IN OTHER DOMAINS (CONT'D)

APPROACHES TO LEARNING *and* SCIENCE	Chooses to participate in an increasing variety of tasks and activities, developing the ability to make independent choices.	Approaches tasks and activities with increased flexibility, imagination, and inventivenes.	Grows in eagerness to learn about and discuss a growing range of topics, ideas, and tasks.	Grows in abilities to set goals and persist in and complete a variety of tasks, activities, and projects, despite distractions or interruptions.	Develops increasing ability to find more than one solution to a question, task, or problem.	Grows in recognizing and solving problems through active exploration, interactions, and discussions with peers and adults.
Explores/questions—Engages in open-ended explorations; forms questions that guide actions.	✓	✓	✓	✓		✓
Begins to investigate—Engages in simple investigations to extend observations, test predictions, and pursue questions.	✓	✓	✓	✓	✓	✓
Collects data—Uses senses, varied tools, and simple measures to gather data.		✓	✓		✓	✓
Records and represents experience—Describes and records experiences and information through a variety of means, including two- and three-dimensional representation, charts, and movement.	✓	✓	✓	✓	✓	
Synthesizes and analyzes data from experiences—Sees patterns in data and relationships among experiences; makes reasonable predictions, explanations, and generalizations based on experience.			✓	✓	✓	✓
Uses language to communicate findings—Develops increased vocabulary and ability to communicate observations and ideas.			✓	✓		✓
Collaborates—Shares materials, tasks, and ideas; collaborates in joint investigations.		✓			✓	✓

index

The Young Scientist series was developed by a team of early childhood and science educators from the Tool Kit for Early Childhood Science Education project at Education Development Center, Inc. (EDC) and was funded by a grant from the National Science Foundation. The project was led by Ingrid Chalufour from the Center for Children and Families and Karen Worth from the Center for Science Education. Listed below are the key members of the team, all of whom contributed substantially to the work from its conceptualization to the final product.

INGRID CHALUFOUR, a project director at EDC's Center for Children and Families, has designed and conducted professional development programs for staff in child care programs, Head Start, public schools, and social service agencies for more than thirty-five years and is a principal developer of the Excellence in Teaching programs.

SHARON GROLLMAN, a senior research associate at EDC's Center for Children and Families, has developed educational materials for more than twenty years. Prior to coming to EDC, she was part of a research team in early childhood.

ROBIN MORIARTY is a research associate at EDC's Center for Science Education. Her work includes curriculum development, leading professional development programs, and working with early childhood centers. She taught young children in the Boston area for fourteen years before she joined EDC.

JEFFREY WINOKUR is a senior research associate at EDC's Center for Science Education. His work includes curriculum development and leading professional development programs for early childhood and elementary science education. He has worked in early childhood and science education for over twenty years and is an instructor in education at Wheelock College.

KAREN WORTH is a senior scientist at EDC's Center for Science Education. Her work includes the development of science curriculum and professional development programs, as well as consultation in science education for young children. She is also a graduate-level instructor at Wheelock College in the early childhood education department and has worked in the field of science and early childhood education for the past thirty-five years.